KT-469-952

THE ATLAS OF
TRAIN TRAVEL
J. B. HOLLINGSWORTH

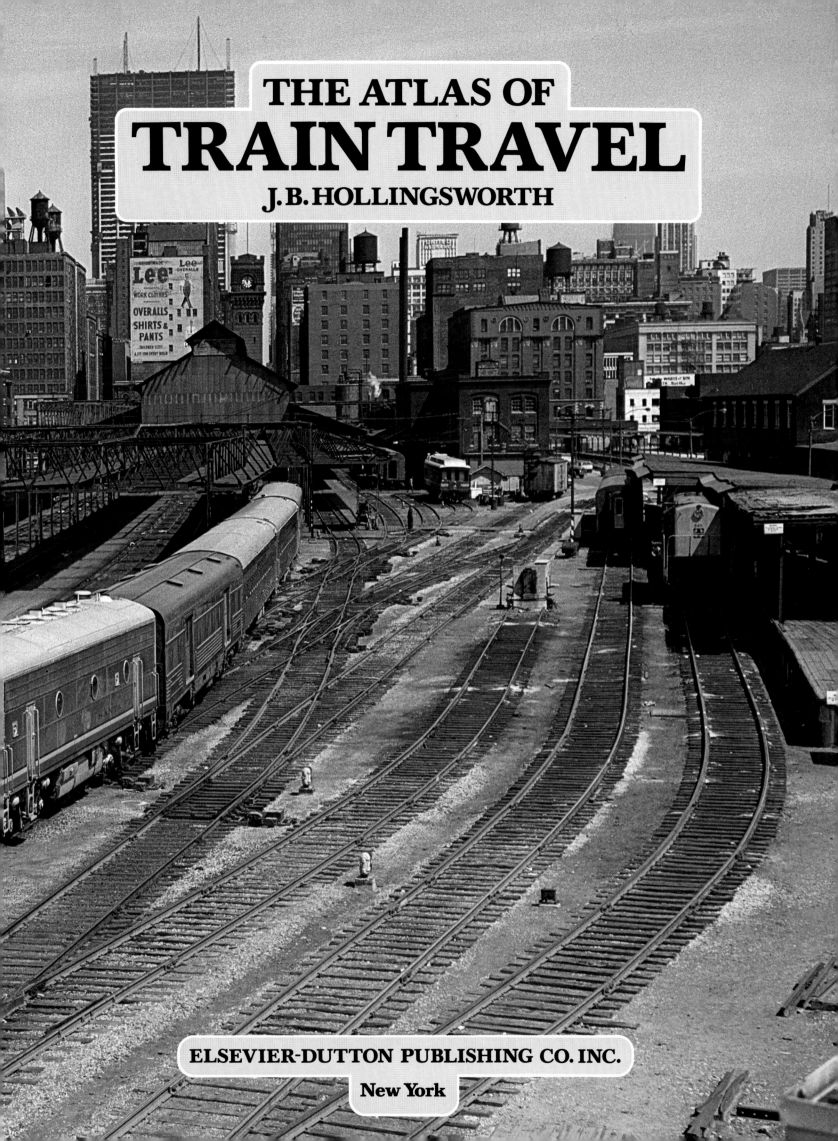

THE ATLAS OF
TRAIN TRAVEL

J. B. HOLLINGSWORTH

ELSEVIER-DUTTON PUBLISHING CO. INC.

New York

Published by
Elsevier-Dutton Publishing Co. Inc.
2 Park Avenue,
New York,
N.Y. 10016.

© Copyright 1980 Basinghall Books Limited

Produced by
Basinghall Books Limited,
59 Cambridge Road,
Kings Heath,
Birmingham, England.

All rights reserved. No part of this publication
may be reproduced, stored in a retrieval system,
or transmitted in any form by any means, electronic,
mechanical, photocopying, recording or otherwise,
without the permission of the publishers and the
copyright holders.

ISBN 0-525-70726-3
Library of Congress Catalogue No 80-65590

Editor: Janet Maclennan
Designer: Derek Copsey
Maps: Peter Cannings

Printed in Hong Kong

Contents

Introduction

It is the intention of this book to describe the flavor of rail travel in different parts of the world. The book is certainly not a timetable, nor is it intended to be a travel guide; but it does on occasion point out, in what the author hopes is a light-hearted way, some of the 'dos and don'ts' a traveller should have in mind when considering plans to see the world by rail. The marvellous past of rail travel is not ignored, but there is no question of tantalizing the reader with vanished glories – only when the present has something which compensates for the past (as is usually the case), is nostalgia allowed free rein.

Of course, one is spoiled for choice. Several books could be filled with descriptions of routes that are equally as good as the ones chosen here. Covering the railways of the world would be a lifetime's occupation. There are more than 700,000 miles of railroad offering passenger service in the world today, so if one travelled 1500 new miles a week for three months each year, it could be done in 30 years! Hence, of the experiences recorded in this volume, some are fresh (eg, India, Pakistan) but with a backward glance over the shoulder at the past. Others, while not going back that *full* 30 years, are less recent; in these there is a forward look to the present day. Yet other lines are so familiar from everyday travel that the only way to deal with a journey is rather less personally . . . .

Twenty journeys or routes have been picked out on the basis that I and my collaborators have liked them and want to share them with you. Allowing that one devotes three weeks or a month each year entirely to train travel, one could cover them comfortably in a mere seven years or so! Incidentally, the order in which they are set out is entirely on the basis of respect for old age; thus, Great Britain, which introduced steam railways in 1825 comes first, and China which waited until 1883, comes last.

The itineraries are based on schedules current at the time of writing; anyone who tries them out will first have to check that no awkward changes have been made.

Brian Hollingsworth

Why Take the Train

Collect a trunk load of travel brochures from your friendly local travel agent and you will discover that a minute fraction will include even a mention of journeys by rail. Yet rail travel compares favorably with air travel in many important ways – there are the pleasures of being able to jump on a train almost on impulse without telling anyone beforehand, of not having to be strapped in, of being able to have one's luggage with one and, finally of course, actually disembarking *at* one's destination instead of at an airfield miles outside (though it must be admitted that in the USA some of these good qualities, including the last, no longer exist).

It is also fair to say that some of the problems inherent in the world's recent social and technological 'progress' – *viz*; high-jacking, and problems brought about by unfamiliarity with sophisticated technology – affect trains less often than airliners. Trains operate more regularly in bad weather; they are also several times safer than airplanes, but this last has no real significance, for the dangers involved in either method of transport are negligible.

Nicely balanced between *pro* and *con* is the matter of eating on trains. Nothing is nicer than making one's way along the train to the diner and choosing something tasty from the menu (and remember that good food served on a train tastes superb and even moderate food tastes good). On the other hand, as the restaurant car is a separate coach, it sometimes gets detached or never put on. The airlines may offer take-it-or-leave-it re-heated food at your cramped seat, but at least the pantry is integral with the aircraft.

The main *con* in respect of travel by train is that it is rather slow. Typically, station-to-station average speeds are ten times slower than airport to airport ones. Over any distance this dwarfs the fact that railway-platform-to-city-center times are

equally typically some twenty times less than airport-runway-to-city-center ones, especially if you include time to collect baggage. The true train traveller, of course, regards the journey as an end in itself and this *con* accordingly becomes a *pro* – the longer the journey lasts, the better.

Two other things on the debit side must be mentioned. Firstly, rail travel is not normally cheap relative to air. For example, a London firm offering package ski holidays in the Alps can arrange *second-class* rail travel instead of air at around £40 ($80) *extra*. Of course, high individual journey costs can be mitigated by using the 'unlimited travel' passes issued by some countries; they are usually very reasonably priced and are valid over wide areas such as Europe, the United States, India and elsewhere.

A second drawback is that ancient reservation procedures on some railways, unchanged from 'quill pen' days, do sometimes creak a little. At A

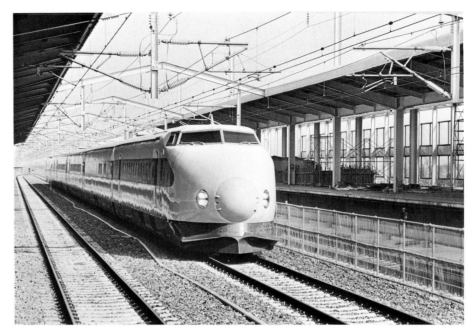

there may be no problem in reserving a seat or berth from A to B; but try asking for a return reservation at short notice from B to A while still at A and there are – on most railways – bad problems. Accordingly sensible travel agents do little to encourage their clients to make any but the simplest journeys by rail. Fortunately not all purveyors of travel are sensible.

But all of these things pale beside the pleasure of having a behind-the-scenes look at the world through a railway carriage window. Unlike viewing the same scene through the window of a car, one does not have to drive, navigate, or superintend the driver from behind: traffic lights and jams are no longer frustrations. Without these mechanical distractions, so many interests – architecture, scenery, agriculture, natural history and so on – can be indulged in up to the hilt. It is this which makes train travel an unequalled way to travel.

Pictures of the opening day of the Stockton & Darlington Railway show, behind *Locomotion*, the travellers making the best of unsprung, loose-coupled chauldron coal wagons. This would represent an extreme of discomfort, as they were unsprung both vertically (the wheels) and horizontally (the buffers). Beyond this, rancid animal fat was used for lubrication and this might spoil the enjoyment even while stationary of what was a fine day and an historic occasion.

Better things were to come – for first-class passengers anyway – when in 1830 the Liverpool and Manchester Railway commenced operations with what were effectively stage-coach 'inside' bodies in threes on four-wheeled rail chassis. This compartment layout, ultimately with eight or more 'bodies' forming each coach, and in due time modernized with a side corridor, remained the norm in Britain and Europe until the 1960s. Early American railroads favored the open coach – which most of the world's railways have now adopted – in which the passengers sit either side of a central aisle, with entrance and exit

Station-to-station speeds in excess of 100mph first came with these now famous Japanese National Railways' 'bullet' trains.

Left:
Steam for pleasure in Britain: Alan Pegler's legendary 4–6–2 *Flying Scotsman* passes Bath on 19 September 1963 with a special Pullman train.

How Rail Comfort Developed

through doors at the ends. Rougher tracks across the Atlantic in the USA led to the mounting of carriage bodies on the now familiar four-wheel trucks or bogies as early as 1840. The present-day layout of railway carriage, therefore, evolved very early and development has taken the form of improvements rather than basic change. Stronger construction and automatic brakes have improved safety; air-conditioning (sometimes), heating and better bogies have improved comfort out of all recognition. One major improvement involved communication between adjacent vehicles. Access to and between open carriages was originally via open and drafty platforms at each end. By the early 1900s these were beginning to be made into closed vestibules and the vehicles joined to one another by flexible corridor connections. This feature is now virtually universal.

May one say as politely as possible that amongst all this, the one improvement that – from the point of view of travellers over any distance – stands out ahead of the others, is the provision of lavatories. Even before corridors came in, the best coaches had little 'utility' rooms leading out of compartments.

Not all changes were improvements; for example, during the 1850s railways in Britain stopped using coke which burns cleanly and began using coal which gives off smoke and smuts. However, anthracite coal was an improvement over the dirty-burning coal originally used. The Delaware, Lackawanna & Western Railroad once even wooed customers with such refrains as . . . .

'Phoebe says and Phoebe knows
That smoke and cinders ruin clothes,
So 'tis a pleasure and delight
To take that road of anthracite'.

(Phoebe Snow gave her name to the Lackawanna's crack express, once an excellent but by no means well-known route from Chicago to New York.) Diesel (and oil-fired steam) traction brought matters back to where they were before, but electric traction has removed even the mild residues that the burning of coke or oil produced.

In the first years of railways, passengers generally either brought their own food or snatched what they could to eat in dining rooms during stops. Similarly, they slept as best they could in carriage seats when overnight journeys were involved. In due time, dining, buffet and sleeping cars evolved to meet these needs.

The first recorded regular provision of sleeping accommodation in trains was well ahead of its general provision. There was a bed carriage on

An immigrant car on the Canadian Pacific Railway – this was the way those from the 'Old World' travelled to their new homes in North America.

Left:
The interior of a Pullman car built in Britain and operated by the Compagnie Internationale des Wagons Lits in Egypt. They were used to form such trains as the 'Star of Egypt' and the 'Luxor Express.'

Below:
A corridor carriage of modern-day France.

the London and Birmingham Railway in 1838, while the first record of a regularly operated public dining car was on the Great Western Railway of Canada (now part of Canadian National), in 1867. Such facilities, as appropriate, are now normal on most overnight and long-distance trains the world over.

Many special types of passenger carriage have existed, such as church cars, library cars, dance cars, observation cars, gymnasium cars, bath cars, and so on, but they give pleasure to the student of quirks and curiosities rather than play a serious role in the evolution of modern passenger transport. An exception is the class of vehicles built for heads of state and other VIPs; in some countries and in the early years what was right for Kings and Queens in one decade became available for their subjects in the next.

Improvement in speed has not been an un-alloyed blessing. In some ways, a fast train gives less value (on a time basis) for money and it is certainly easier to sleep in a slow one. Furthermore, by the nature of things, fast trains and spectacular scenery are not found in combination; this is because the only way one can build a high-speed railway through the mountains is to put it in a tunnel – and tunnels are the most boring bits of scenery one could have.

Such developments and thinking led to the Grand Hotel concept of train travel, developed in the last quarter of the 19th century by Georges Nagelmakers in Europe (and elsewhere) under the immortal title *Compagnie Internationale des Wagons-Lits et des Grands Express Européens*. In America George Pullman did the same, making his name a synonym for luxury, and giving a new word to the English language. Whether called a

Train de-luxe, an All-Pullman Limited or even a Democratic People's Express, a luxury train is required to meet the following specifications:

(a) It must be exclusive: ie, first or 'soft' class only.

(b) If night travel is involved, all passengers must be accommodated in rooms or compartments, each with one, two (or at the very most, three) beds only, made up, of course, at night.

(c) Meals must be impeccably served at tables in a dining car with *à la carte* as well as *table d'hôte* service.

(d) A buffet car and a bar car which serve light refreshments and drinks at all reasonable hours must be available.

(e) A lounge and/or observation car, may be combined with (d), for general socializing en route must be available.

The numbers of trains which met these severe standards reached peaks in 1914, 1929 and 1939, but nowadays they are rare in the extreme. It is believed that only in South Africa and Mexico can they currently be found, as regards regular overnight runs.

Nostalgia for these great trains is only partly the inspiration for this book. It is more correct to say that the theme of it is that we should admire but not weep for the past, when so many wonderful but different trains run for our enjoyment in the present.

A mixed train hauled by a Beyer-Garratt locomotive crosses the famous Victoria Falls Bridge between Zimbabwe and Zambia. Cecil Rhodes himself specified that the carriages should be washed by the spray as they crossed.

Exploring the World by Train

For those with a fair amount of time (and money) on their hands, a globe-trotting expedition by train is one sure way of finding out how the rest of the world lives. Of course, it is not possible to circumnavigate by train, and even assuming that no frontier or line is closed for political reasons, neither is it possible to make uninterrupted train journeys up and down the great land masses of America or Europe–Asia–Africa. But one can go a long way.

The longest continuous journey one could make wholly by rail is the 10,133 miles from a little-known place called Ayamonte in Spain to Ho Chi Minh City (better known as Saigon) in Vietnam.

It involves changing in Seville, Madrid, Paris, Moscow, Peking and Hanoi. Except in Vietnam, sleeping and dining cars are available on the long hauls. Bogies would be changed at the Spanish-French, Polish-USSR and Mongolian-USSR-Chinese frontiers, while passengers are still on board, to take care of differences in the railway gauge. This is fixed at 5ft 6in in Spain, 4ft 8½in in France, Germany and Poland, 5ft 0in in the USSR, 4ft 8½in again in China and 3ft 3⅜in (meter gauge) between Hanoi and Ho Chi Minh.

Ayamonte, on the southernmost point of the frontier with Portugal, is close to the south coast international resorts of the Algarve, but there is no rail connection across the river which forms the frontier. The long journey starts in the morning with a humble railcar (second class) to the famous city of Seville, with a choice of a late evening diesel express or an overnight train (first-class sleepers available) to Madrid Chambertin.

In the early evening the '*Puerta Del Sol*' ('Gateway to the Sun') express departs from the superb (but slightly inaccessible) new Madrid Chambertin Station. Paris Austerlitz is reached the next morning; transfer to Paris Nord is accomplished by the famous Metro. Again, time for a quick sightseeing trip and a meal before departure on the '*Ost-West Express*' at 1713, using the daily Russian Paris-Moscow sleeping car. There is no dining car on this train before it reaches Berlin in the morning, so the suggestion is that the voyageur obtain a hurried Parisian lunch – one that does not continue after 1630 hours – and buy ingredients for a picnic for the evening. The sleeping car attendant should have the samovar in steam for beverages. Two nights and 1½ days later one arrives in Moscow, hopefully in the early afternoon. A slightly dicey connection would (if Intourist, the Russian travel and tourist surveillance agency allow it) enable one to leave – by an un-named train – for Peking at 1725 Tuesdays only. This train runs via Mongolia. However on Fridays only there is a departure at 2040 which runs via Manchuria, a 700-mile longer journey and one that at present runs through quite steamy and humid territory at the far end. Arrival at Peking is, respectively, 1529 the following Monday or 0640 the following Friday.

The Hanoi train leaves Peking in the afternoon, Tuesdays and Saturdays. If one's visas were in order arrival would be in the late evening of the following Thursday or Monday. The real *bonne bouche* comes at the end; the remaining 880 miles to Ho Chi Minh City takes four days, including overnight stops at Hue and Da Nang. The running of this twice-weekly train, although not yet quite in the absolute top league regarding speed and comfort, is very commendable, bearing in mind the almost total destruction of the line in the recent war. The only photograph which has surfaced in the West shows steam traction, a pleasant way to end a journey of almost precisely three weeks.

There is, of course, a possible southern route, extending in principle from Europe to Singapore.

The last spike is driven to complete the line connecting Kenya with Gulu, near the border between Uganda and the Sudan. It is physically (but not politically) possible to travel all the way by train from this point to Cape Town.

13

Right:
The Bridge over the River Kwai marks the present end of track of the Thailand railway system. The grade leading from here over the Three Pagodas Pass into Burma was the notorious 'Death Railway' of World War II, on which many thousands of Allied prisoners died.

Below:
Chinese National Railways: Passengers make use of washing facilities on the station platform after an overnight run from Tientsin to Nanking.

But three major gaps, not now likely to be filled and each of them hundreds of miles in length, rather spoil the tidy concept of such a train voyage. The gaps are: – Kerman in Iran to Zahedan on the border with Pakistan; Dibrugarh in Assam via the Ledo Road to Myitkyina in Burma; over the Three Pagodas Pass from Moulmein in Burma to Nam Tok in Thailand, where ran the notorious, partly graded but never completed, 'Death Railway' of World War II.

West to east on the North and South American continents is commonplace to the extent that there are at least 12 possible non-demanding transcontinental routes – not forgetting the 56 mile Panama Railroad, which once charged $25 in silver dollars for the ride. (See routes 4, 6 and 13.)

North to south in the Americas by train is a little more ambitious, and no doubt one could hypothetically buy a ticket from Churchill, Manitoba (on Hudsons' Bay) to Merida in Mexico. If one travels on to Cuidad Hidalgo near

the Mexico-Guatemala frontier, one can see that the rails continue much farther south, as far as Cutuco in the Republic of El Salvador but no train connections are given across either frontier. From Churchill to Merida, however, one could travel in great comfort the whole way, since sleepers and diners run throughout. Starting in an un-named train (see Route 6), as far as Winnipeg, the traveller can go from Winnipeg by 'Super Continental' to Vancouver, 'Pacific International' to Seattle, 'Coast Starlight' to Los Angeles, 'Sunset Limited' to El Paso, 'El Fronterizo' to Mexico City, 'El Meridano' to Merida. Scenery with a capital 'S' graces a high proportion of the 6340-mile journey.

To go further one has to do quite a lot of republic-hopping before joining Ken Mills' excellent itinerary (Route 13), describing continuous rails from Bolivia down to the extreme south-end of the continent.

In Europe-Asia-Africa, the north to south journey came very much closer to being a reality. Starting in the north of Norway at Narvik a train ferry takes the train between Sweden and Denmark or Germany. Alas, although a train ferry does cross to Asia at Istanbul, it does not carry loaded passenger cars. Again, standard-gauge railway tracks have existed and a rail formation does exist all the way from Istanbul to Egypt, but almost all the countries concerned are at present quarrelling with their neighbors. The Suez Canal Authorities, too, whether French, British or Egyptian, have always been unwilling to allow a railway bridge across their thoroughfare except when forced to during the two World Wars.

Southwards from Cairo, the River Nile provides two undoubtedly pleasant – and certainly educational – interludes from rail travel, largely in railway-owned steamers. These sectors, totalling 1200 miles, are the physical gaps in the 6500-mile route. From Pakwach on the Nile in troubled Uganda, an all-rail route exists via Nairobi, Dar-es-Salaam, Lusaka, Bulawayo, Mafeking and Kimberley to Cape Town. Through-carriages are not, however, worked across the famous bridge at the Victoria Falls ('the carriages washed by the spray' as Cecil Rhodes intended) nor at present are there any trains between Kenya and Tanzania. Also, no train or even streetcar connects the old and new stations in Dar-es-Salaam.

Perhaps these ultimate theoretical journeys are ones which no one will ever make. However, lots of people manage the elements of which they are composed; many of these, together with others, are described in a more personal way in the body of the book. But although these words have been set down only a few days, already travel across Iran and from China to Vietnam has become problematical. One must remember that although the barriers to free travel of physical difficulty, time, and cost have been largely dismantled over the last two hundred years, plenty of manmade obstacles remain. It was only during the brief Golden Age of the 19th century that these seemed to disappear.

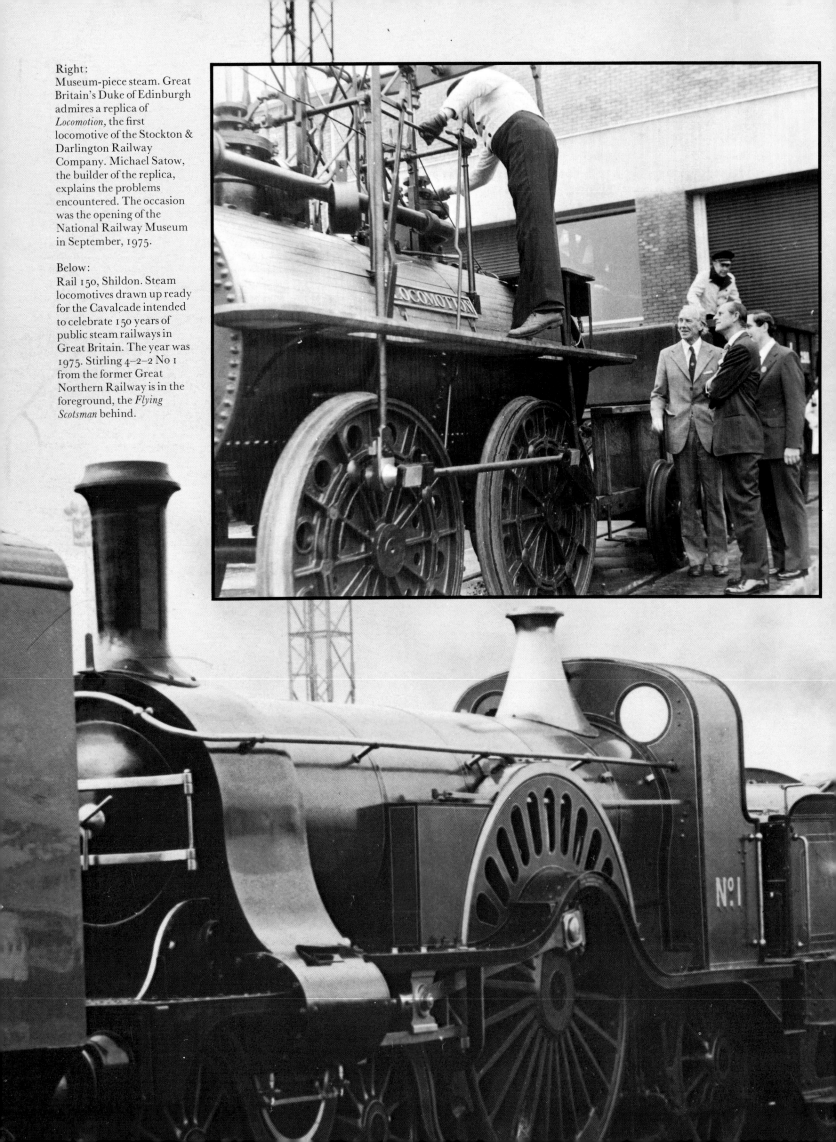

Right:
Museum-piece steam. Great Britain's Duke of Edinburgh admires a replica of *Locomotion*, the first locomotive of the Stockton & Darlington Railway Company. Michael Satow, the builder of the replica, explains the problems encountered. The occasion was the opening of the National Railway Museum in September, 1975.

Below:
Rail 150, Shildon. Steam locomotives drawn up ready for the Cavalcade intended to celebrate 150 years of public steam railways in Great Britain. The year was 1975. Stirling 4–2–2 No 1 from the former Great Northern Railway is in the foreground, the *Flying Scotsman* behind.

This book appears at a sad moment for the railway lover; the reason is that the steam locomotive, most evocative of all the elements which went to make up a railway, is dying out. Thirty short years ago, the steam traction fleet of mankind numbered some 400,000; placed (inevitably) end-to-end, they would stretch comfortably across North America. But now most are gone; in fact, only 20,000 or so remain in the world while these words are being written; by the time they are printed, fires will have been finally dropped on a sizeable proportion of even this vestigial remnant.

The shock of this sudden occurrence has done two things. Survivors, even in the most inaccessible corners, are being searched for while there is yet time (and those who do this, incidentally, often find themselves welcomed as only happens in places where tourists seldom go). At the same time, when steam gets shelved in one particular country, the sad event triggers off an explosion of nostalgia on the part of railway enthusiasts, professional and otherwise. So we find new railway museums being created and old ones being enlarged. But more and more it is being recognized that steam locomotives need fires in their grates if what they once were is to be remembered.

The idea of actually running museum-piece obsolete main-line locomotives for nostalgic reasons seems to have originated with a body called the Railway Correspondence and Travel Society who in 1938 chartered a 'special' from London to Cambridge to be hauled by Stirling 8ft single 4–2–2 No 1. The London & North Eastern Railway had recently brought it out from the museum as a publicity stunt in connection with new rolling stock for the 'Flying Scotsman' train. The enthusiasts of the time had a great day out. . . . 40 years later, such an event is commonplace, as we shall see.

At that time, the idea of some private person buying main-line locomotives to run would have been thought absurd. It was only thought possible if they did it in miniature – until Alan Pegler came along and bought (for not much more than the price of a good family car) the 'Flying Scotsman' locomotive. In fact (to set the records straight) he was not the first to buy a *full-size* locomotive: the first was Bill Smith who acquired an 0–6–0 T of Great Northern Railway origin a year earlier.

Since then the pendulum has swung back from private ownership. Taxes and inflation have made it just too costly (as Alan Pegler's bankruptcy demonstrated in a vivid and tragic way), and bigger, less personal organizations are taking over, now that the path-finding has been done.

Another big influence, but a gradual rather than a sudden one, was the closure of personable little railways, usually of gauges narrower than Stephenson's standard. They were the kind that were almost too quaint to compete with the donkey, but always waited for Mrs Jones to finish her shopping. Some abortive attempts at rescue were made in the United States before World War II, but it was left to a man called Ellis D Attwood, to pioneer what has now become a worldwide industry.

Railway Nostalgia: Museums and Revivals

As the war ended, Attwood, who had acquired four locomotives and much else from defunct 2ft gauge railroads in the State of Maine, began building a railroad on his farm. It was formed as a circuit, $5\frac{1}{2}$ miles in length, the dykes between the cranberry bogs providing ready-made grades on which he and his men could spike down the second-hand rails he had bought. His original idea was that it should provide essential transport for the estate and only on high days and holidays be a pleasure line for himself and his friends, a thought which smacked a little of the father who brings home a train set 'for the lad.' Anyone for miles around who had even begun to think trains were nice things started to clamor for an invitation. Before long, public demand on the one hand and heavy costs on the other influenced EDA to throw the line open as a public spectacle. In this way EDAville and, indeed, the whole concept of steam railways for pleasure, were born.

Monday 7 April 1947 was the day when the final and golden spike was ceremoniously driven at noon on the Edaville Railroad. Since that auspicious day, Edaville – and railway preservation round the world – has gone from strength to strength. The operation, although not accessible by rail, is situated 45 miles from Boston at a place called South Carver. It is in an area which includes famous Plymouth Rock and Cape Cod, traditional magnets for visitors who now often put Edaville on their itinerary.

The 2ft 3in gauge Talyllyn Railway at Towyn, Wales (which we shall be visiting in our first itinerary) was the first railway to be taken over by amateurs as a going (if that is the word) concern. This take-over occurred in 1951 and, surprisingly, to onlookers (as well as a few participants) has been completely successful.

Since then, 200 or so other nostalgia railways have sprung up in the world, on the majority of which live steam locomotives can be found. The whole story is told in much detail in the book *Steam for Pleasure* (Routledge and Kegan Paul of London and Boston, 1978) written jointly by John Snell, Patrick Whitehouse (both also associated with this book) and the present writer.

How to Travel by Train

A must for any potential traveller is a certain book of ordinary size – the 550-page monthly *Thomas Cook International Timetable of Railway and Local Shipping Services*. To a dedicated railway enthusiast the most laconic of its entries conjures up a vivid picture of some great train rolling towards the sunset.

Three years ago the press and television covered one particular non-event, the demise of the 'Orient Express.' However, if one consults the current copy of Cook's timetable, there in table 32 is set out the schedule of the 'Orient Express,' still running between Paris (Est) and Bucharest, the same termini that it connected on its first run in 1883. The media got hold of the wrong train! (An explanation is given in Chapter III.)

A study of back numbers of Cook's timetable indicates that rail travel in the past was not necessarily better than today's. For example, the superb trains that now run between London and South Wales or Tokyo and Osaka, compare very favorably with the very second-rate ones which operated on these routes a few years ago. At the same time, the service now offered on, say, the aforementioned 'Orient Express' or between Chicago and Los Angeles is poor compared with what was available in the day of *trains de-luxe* or the 'Super Chief' respectively.

It may be noted that rail facilities can have merit in more than one way. On the one hand, many will commend a German train, say, on the grounds of its comfort, speed and observance of the timetable. On the other, a journey in, say, Paraguay, where the train's time-keeping and even its running is so erratic that the timetable is not worth publishing, may also get the equivalent of a gold medal – a puff of steam, perhaps – because of its museum-piece carriages and steam-age relic of a locomotive. The merits of both receive attention.

It was said earlier that a drawback to rail travel

is the problem of making reservations. The answer? Well, if young and carefree then a night spent standing in the corridor is no worry, should the worst come to the worst. But if one is older and values one's comfort, it is unfortunate that good judgment and encyclopedic knowledge (of everything from railway practices to Saints' days and football results) are needed before one can predict with confidence whether, on a particular train on a particular day, a chance-traveller would be jammed in the corridor or spoiled for choice between a dozen empty, clean and spacious compartments.

A solution which cuts the Gordian Knot of this problem is to sample the wares of various people who offer packaged rail travel. Many firms and societies offer such facilities; mostly, they advertise in the English periodicals *Railway Magazine* and *Railway World* or the American magazine *Trains*. Thomas Cook (who began business over 100 years ago by offering excursions by train) is still in the forefront.

Three types of rail tour can be recognized.

First, one put together to special order by a travel agent who is used to coping with the vagaries of railway companies.

The second type of rail tour consists of a fixed package of railway interest for a group, led by someone with some knowledge of the area to be visited.

The third is the live-in-the-train type of tour. The range here goes from old-fashioned de-luxe on Herr Glatt's new 'Orient Express' to do-it-yourself-in-a-loincloth on an Indian Railways 'tourist coach.' It is not surprising that there is a 20 to 1 price variation per night between the two. Of course, there are others at more sensible prices in between. An all-steam tour of South Africa (qv) is such a one.

The other main drawback of rail travel – the time taken – can also be mitigated by such things as a wise choice of companion(s), books, games and refreshment; and, in respect of the passing scene, a curiosity both lively and informed. Making a traveller so informed is a main aim of this book.

The 'life-in-the-train' type of rail tour – a South African Railways' 'Steam Safari' train ascends the northern slope of the Montagu Pass behind a class GMA Beyer-Garratt in November 1979.

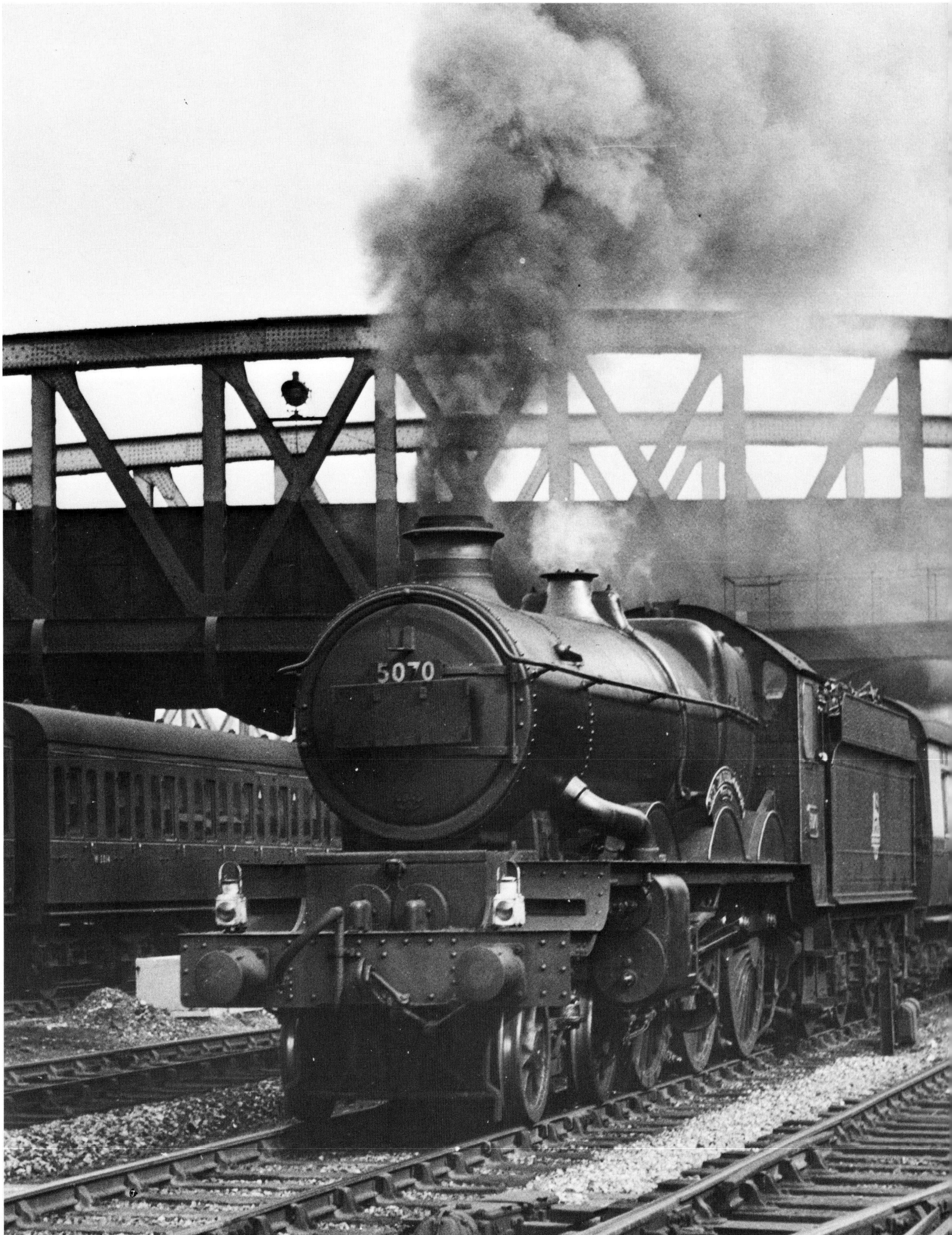
5070

Great Britain

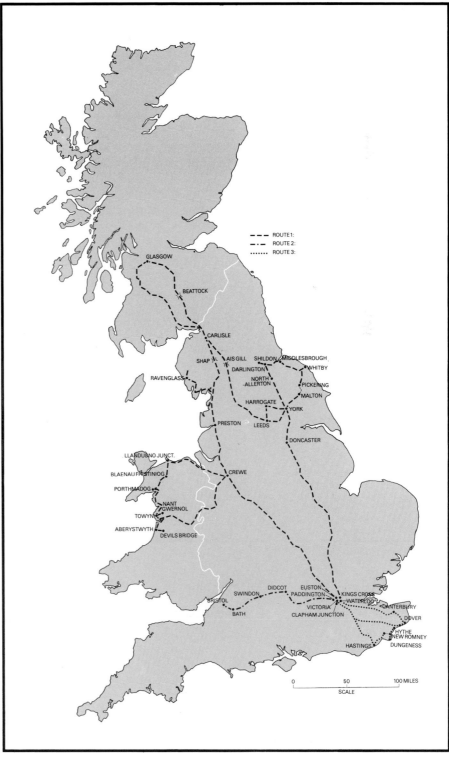

ROUTE 1: — — —
ROUTE 2: — · — ·
ROUTE 3: · · · · · ·

GLASGOW

BEATTOCK

CARLISLE

SHAP
AIS GILL
SHILDON
MIDDLESBROUGH
DARLINGTON
WHITBY
NORTH -ALLERTON
PICKERING
RAVENGLASS
MALTON
HARROGATE
YORK
PRESTON
LEEDS
DONCASTER

LLANDUDNO JUNCT.

BLAENAU FFESTINIOG
CREWE
PORTHMADOG
NANT GWERNOL
TOWYN
ABERYSTWYTH
DEVILS BRIDGE

SWINDON
DIDCOT
EUSTON
BRISTOL
PADDINGTON
KINGS CROSS
WATERLOO
CANTERBURY
BATH
VICTORIA
DOVER
CLAPHAM JUNCTION
HYTHE
NEW ROMNEY
HASTINGS
DUNGENESS

0   50   100 MILES
SCALE

As might be expected of the country in which railways originated, the people of Britain have an extravagant passion for trains. Passenger services are maintained well above any reasonable economic level, despite some well-publicized and lamented cutbacks, and nostalgic railway activities are indulged in to a degree unmatched in any other country. There are over 200 railway museums, preserved railways and such in Britain. World inter-city travel by steam train began in 1830 when the railway between Liverpool and Manchester was opened to the public. Twenty years later all the principal cities of Britain were inter-connected by rail. Sleeping cars were available from 1848 and restaurant cars from 1895. Corridor trains arrived in 1892. The privately owned lines were nationalized in 1947 and since that time British Railways has run the majority of trains operated in the United Kingdom.

Fast running has always been a feature; even as early as 1850 trains were running between London and Bristol at an average start-to-finish speed of 46mph. Nowadays BR have by far the fastest trains to run on other-than-electrified lines; on electrified lines the Advanced Passenger Train (APT) – expected to come into service during 1980 – will give even higher average speeds. Many trains are today booked at start-to-stop average speeds of more than 85mph.

Over the last 20 years a fleet of 18,000 steam locomotives of 800 different types have been replaced by 5000 diesel and electric ones of a mere 30 or so designs. More than 43,000 passenger carriages have decreased to 16,000 and the route-mileage on which they work has been reduced from 18,000 to 9000. In spite of this diminution, the system remains fascinating and heavily used. Two and one-half million people still travel by rail each working day. All trains except a few commuter runs have first- and second-class accommodation. 'Open' carriages are currently taking over from the 'compartment' type although this process has gone further in second class than in first. There is little difference in comfort between the two classes – greater exclusivity is the reward of buying the more expensive ticket. Incidentally, would-be explorers of BR are recommended to buy the Britrail pass, an all-stations unlimited-travel ticket, available for periods between one week and one month to non-Britons.

Most long-distance day trains have a buffet car and on many there is restaurant service as well. There are sleeping cars (first class with single-berth compartments, second with double) on many overnight trains. All sleeping berths have made-up beds with sheets and each compartment has a wash basin.

In general services are frequent. For example between London Euston and Birmingham there is a high-speed buffet-car train every 30 minutes except on one day, the dreaded railway Sunday. Sundays before 3 pm are reserved for repairing the lines and trains then are infrequent, slow and most unreliable. The reader must consider himself or herself warned.

A Morecambe–Glasgow train takes water at the Tebay Water Troughs. The locomotive is a 'Black Five' 4–6–0.

Route 1
Locomotion
and All That

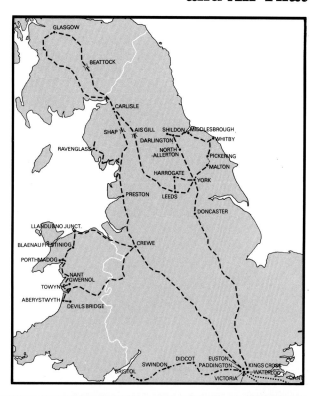

It can all be said to have begun when (as the plaque on the old station house at Stockton, County Durham, England, puts it), 'HERE IN 1825 THE STOCKTON AND DARLINGTON RAILWAY COMPANY BOOKED THE FIRST PASSENGER THUS MARKING AN EPOCH IN THE HISTORY OF MANKIND.' Actually, the Stockton & Darlington set another fine railway tradition by never (not even on the opening day) running between its two namesakes; in fact it ran from collieries near Bishop Auckland to the tide-water at Stockton. It just happened to pass through the then-outskirts of Darlington. The claim of the S & D to be the first public passenger railway in the world with (some) steam haulage is not contested, but it should be added that except on the opening day, only coal trains were steam-hauled and this remained so for years. Even so, a Stockton & Darlington excursion claims pride of place in this book, and a good deal of the original line can still be enjoyed.

One also starts with two of British Rail's best items: the HST 125 (High Speed Train – 125mph) and breakfast. All passengers should proceed to Kings Cross station (London) for the 0740 Edinburgh train. It is wise to have reserved seats.

Incidentally a third nice thing about BR is that

the drinking hours which apply elsewhere in Britain do not apply on trains so one can 'down his first pint' long before the more permanently situated pubs and bars are allowed to open.

One odd thing about HST trains is that they bear an extraordinary resemblance to the London & North Eastern streamlined steam trains introduced on this route in 1935 and are just as revolutionary. Running time then to Darlington was 195 minutes whereas it is now 164 minutes. Impressive, however, was the fact that the time from commencing design work on the 1935 train until entering revenue service was six months, not six years as it was with the HST.

Anyway, soon enough the HST125 is rolling out of London's northern suburbs with BR's new (1977) electrification; it calls to pick up passengers at Stevenage, passes Hitchin and Huntingdon and then crosses the black earth of the marshy fens. Fenland people are widely supposed to be born with webbed feet – confirmation, if true, of the theory of mankind's aquatic origin, so well set out in Elaine Morgan's fascinating book *Descent of Woman*. Then we race through Peterborough – 4–6–2s *Silver Link*, *Silver Fox*, *Silver King* and *Quicksilver* on the 1935 'Silver Jubilee' streamliner had to slow down to 20mph to negotiate the curves of the old station here.

After Peterborough comes the climb of the 1 in 200 Stoke Bank, which definitely separated the men from the boys in steam days, but which this amply-powered Chevy Chase hardly seems to notice. Stoke tunnel marks the top of the hill as well as the fact that one is now 100 miles from Kings Cross, negotiated in just over the hour. Grantham, where engines were often changed in steam days, followed by Doncaster where they were built, both go by in a flash. Selby, which has a swing bridge across the River Ouse, requires a severe reduction of speed and there is another at Chaloners Whin Junction on the outskirts of York, where the train is due at 0950.

Time later to admire the magnificent curved station roof at York for at 0952 one takes to the long straight racing ground across the plain of York. The 'Half-Way London-Edinburgh' sign is seen 11.5 miles north of York. Thirsk (where, author and television series hero, veterinary surgeon 'James Herriot,' still has his practise) and Northallerton (where the mayor used to be head of a section gang on the permanent way) pass rapidly by.

At 1024 the HST train is due at Bank Top station, Darlington. The course of the Stockton & Darlington Railway is about a mile away to the north, crossing the main line by what was once a

Left:
An Inter-City 125 High Speed Train enters Kings Cross station.

Below:
A class A4 4–6–2, with a front end strikingly similar to the HST 125 trains of today, leaves the notorious Gas Works tunnel just outside Kings Cross station with the 'Flying Scotsman.'

Right:
Obtained from the National
Coal Board, 0–6–2 T No 29
rouses the echoes as it
climbs from Grosmont to
Goathland on the North
Yorkshire Moors Railway.

Bottom:
The working replica of
Stephenson's *Locomotion* is
prepared for the Loco-
motive Cavalcade staged in
celebration of the 150th
anniversary of steam public
railways.

Below:
A replica train hauled by
the actual *Locomotion* (but
propelled by a gasoline
engine in the tender) leaves
Stockton for Darlington
during the Railway Cen-
tenary Celebrations of 1925.

right-angle crossing. If you take the 1042 Bishop
Auckland diesel train (of a very different order
to the one you have just travelled on), it turns left
shortly after leaving and joins what must ap-
proximate to the original course. North Road
station, Darlington, now the S & D museum,
marks the site of the original S & D station, while
the next stop, Heighington, has the original
building; it is also the place where Stephenson's
famous *Locomotion* was first put on rails. Between
here and Shildon in 1975 was held the Rail 150
Cavalcade, with a replica of *Locomotion* leading,
and the prototype High Speed Train bringing up
the rear; 18 other steam (and one electric)
locomotives paraded in between.

After Shildon the present railway diverges from
the old course but one could walk over the original
route – except where it goes through British
Rail's Wagon Works (via rope-worked inclines to
the pits at Haggerleases that were originally the
sources of the S & D's traffic). Timothy Hack-
worth's original locomotive works is also here.

Returning by train from Shildon one should
alight at North Road station; the relics on display
include the legendary *Locomotion* and another

early S & D locomotive, the 0–6–0 *Derwent*. A
2–4–0 and an 0–6–0 from the S & D's successor,
the North Eastern Railway, are also present.

If it is too long to wait for the next hourly train,
a bus or taxi will take the traveller across town to
Bank Top for another diesel train ride. Being
rather old, these local train sets are not luxurious,
but they are superb for sightseeing; from a front
seat one can see along the line as well as out each
side. A half-hourly service gives one freedom to
take refreshment if desired . . . but take a train to
Middlesbrough, NOT one to Stockton.

The train departs towards the south, turns east
immediately, but does not join the course of the
old S & D (now a siding serving BR's permanent-
way depot) until after Dinsdale, the first stop. We
turn north at Eaglescliffe, then east again over the
River Tees and disembark at Thornaby station
in the heart of industrial Teesside. All this except
the final half-mile follows the original course.
From Thornaby it is a short walk (turn right outside the station) along the main road to the small
building on the left side, just across the river,
which was the Stockton & Darlington's Stockton
station. The claim made that a 'new epoch in the
history of mankind' opened here is, to this writer's
mind, no exaggeration. Incidentally, the present
Stockton station is a good 1.5 miles away on
another line.

The half-hourly wait between trains is just
comfortable time for this little pilgrimage and it is
only one station on, past the great yards serving
Teesside industry, to Middlesbrough for the
Whitby train at 1640; this will take the passenger
away from some of the ugliest vistas in the world
to some of the finest.

The English rural branch line was a perfect
thing – Doctor Beeching (a most reasonable man)
is always blamed for having axed most of them,
but in fact he just happened to arrive at the time
when the plan to do so was being implemented. A
few survive on taxpayers' bounty and of those few
none is more typical or more lovely than the Esk
Valley Line on which we shall travel to Whitby.
It is best to get into the train at the back – the
nicest bits are after Battersby where it reverses.
The train is due just after six o'clock at the little
Yorkshire port of Whitby where in 1768 Captain
Cook set sail in his ship *Endeavour* (which was
built in the town) to explore the world. But that is
recent history as far as Whitby is concerned – in
664 a religious conference called the Synod of
Whitby took place. It was a milestone of Chris-
tianity, whereby for almost 1000 years the English
Church accepted the authority of Rome. Whitby
is a pleasant place in which to spend the night,
and is well provided with hotels.

A propos of BR branch lines, their proliferation
was such that four, no less, served Whitby. A line
from Scarborough came in over the great viaduct
across the valley and there was a second route
from Middlesbrough beside the one we used. BR
also closed the line across the moors to Pickering
(and thence York), but a group of people including many professional railwaymen have re-

opened it as a tourist pleasure railway. This line brings to life old traditional ways of railway working and is staffed largely by volunteers. The North Yorkshire Moors Railway leaves BR (more correct to say that BR leaves it, for the Whitby and Pickering Railway was opened first in 1836) at Grosmont station. Steam trains are run more frequently at week-ends but in any case it is a wonderful scenic ride up to Goathland and across the moors. Even the NYMR diesel trains are packaged under the label 'National Park Scenic Cruise.' The end of the line (and its headquarters) is the attractive little town of Pickering, another place where 20 years ago four lines met, but now only one remains.

So it is a bus for us to Malton, where we can take a train for York (or continue by bus). York is full of hotels; the most convenient one is BR's own Royal Station Hotel (actually part of the station) but it is on the expensive side, although good value. York is an ancient walled city which once rivalled London politically and Canterbury ecclesiastically. The Castle Museum, with its replica streets and shops, is superb, but the whole city itself is one great museum, dominated by the magnificent Cathedral known as the Minster, begun in 1220 and completed 250 years later. Viking influence is shown in that the city streets are called 'gates' – for example Castlegate – while the city gates are called 'bars.' The seven railway lines which radiated from York (including one still independent, the Derwent Valley Railway), all still exist and York harbors what is without doubt the world's Number One railway museum close to the station. The National Railway Museum allows some of its 33 steam locomotives to haul specials on a 65-mile circular route via Harrogate and Leeds; in 1978 and 1979 they ran on summer Sunday mornings and afternoons, but it is necessary to book well ahead. If the arrangements are the same when you come to make this trip (but you must enquire – Cook's timetable

A 4–6–2, No 46203 *Princess Margaret Rose*, at grips with the Beattock Bank incline.

gives the details in advance), then it would be appropriate to set off from London on a Friday; Saturdays are 'steamier' on the North Yorkshire Moors Railway, too.

The treat for Monday is a ride in an ordinary BR locomotive-hauled express over the most scenic main line in England, crossing the Pennine hills ('the backbone of England') in spectacular fashion. It is an early start by either the 0758 or 0816 trains to Leeds (a 45-minute trip) with a view to catching the 0915 buffet-car train from Leeds to Glasgow via Carlisle. The Settle and Carlisle Railway, as it is called, was built in the 1870s to compete with the two older established routes, for the lucrative traffic between England and Scotland. With electrification between London and Glasgow via Crewe, the Settle and Carlisle line has degenerated into secondary status, but this in no way affects its prime position as a spectacle. BR chose this route for its ceremonial 'last' steam train in 1968; other nostalgic 'last' steam trains continue to be run ten years later, but not on a regular basis.

Carlisle Citadel station 'under the wires' is reached in a couple of hours from Leeds. Once upon a time 'blackberry black' London & North Western locomotives, coming from London's Euston, would be changed for polished blue Caledonian Railway ones, to go on to Glasgow; on our line crimson-lake 4–4–0s of the Midland would give way to the elegant dark green machinery of the Glasgow and South Western Railway. Nowadays our diesel locomotive continues on by this G & SW line to Glasgow, diverging from the main electrified route at Gretna Junction, close to the Scottish border point. Gretna, until fairly recently, was the objective of eloping English lovers. Under Scottish law a couple has merely to declare before a witness that they are man and wife and it is so; tradition provided that the blacksmith at Gretna Green performed this office for the runaways, standing by his anvil.

Glasgow could provide a jumping off point for a tour of Scotland's scenic wonders by rail. There is the West Highland Line to Fort William and Mallaig, whence by steamer or bus and ferry north to Kyle of Lochalsh. A lonely but lovely line still runs from here across the Highlands to Inverness; trains run from Inverness both by day and by night directly back into England.

Another option is to take a late afternoon electric express going south. In the very near future BR's newest operating service, the Advanced Passenger Train or APT should be operating. It is not now intended to run the APT at faster maximum speeds than the HST, but the automatic body tilting mechanism allows for faster running on curves – hence, high average speeds without the need to build a new railway. Political and labour-relations (even a few technical) problems have delayed this project from BR's original (and confidently) announced date of 1972 for its introduction; but better late than never, and obviously a 'must' for us.

There is a temptation to alight at Preston to see the only non-museum trams (streetcars) in Britain, at the nearby seaside resort of Blackpool, 'famed for fresh air and fun.' Another possibility is a trip on one of the regular BR steam excursions northwards along the coast to Carnforth, where there is a railway museum, and Ravenglass, where there is a famous 15in gauge miniature steam railway running up into the hills. It is recommended that in Blackpool one should stay at one of the resort's legendary private boarding-houses rather than a hotel.

South of Preston, a few miles south of Wigan station, we pass under an insignificant railway bridge which carried the first inter-city railway in the world, from Liverpool to Manchester. Celebrations reminiscent of those between Darlington and Shildon five years earlier were held for the 150th anniversary of its opening in 1830. One feature was the running of replicas of several of the original locomotives including, of course, Stephenson's *Rocket*.

Below:
A National Park Scenic Cruise.
Diesel Train at Levisham station on the North Yorkshire Moor Railway.

Bottom:
A Doubleheaded Express en route from Glasgow to Mallaig hauled by two class 5 4–6–0s on British Rail's West Highland Line.

No railway circuit of Britain could omit the trains of Wales and, coming from the north, the gateway to Wales is one of the most famous railway junctions and towns of the world . . .

Oh, Mr. Porter,
What shall I do?
I wanted to go to Birmingham
But got carried on to Crewe. . . .

sang Marie Lloyd in the early days of the century. Never was it more appropriate than today. Crewe, though electrified, is still a confusing warren of a place. Trains go in every direction and difficulty is often experienced in trying to find out correct platforms and times.

One of the six sets of tracks radiating away from the station leads to Shrewsbury, a town steeped in history and the need to defend England's borders – known as the Marches – from marauding Welsh tribesmen. For Romans, Anglo-Saxons and Normans, Shrewsbury was a strong-point, so of course there is a castle and, in addition, streets of ancient half-timbered black and white houses sheltering under its skirts.

West of Shrewsbury is a wonderful run on a single line that was once the main line of the old Cambrian railways. The country becomes increasingly wild and the names decreasingly pronounceable as we go on. Again we have panoramic views from our diesel train, which we must leave at a strange V-shaped station, romantically situated in a salt marsh surrounded by the changeless Welsh hills. Dovey Junction is one of those rare and enticing railway stations that exist just for themselves – that is, the only way to reach them is by train, or by walking along the track.

The Pwllheli train leaves at once for its long cruise northwards along a lovely 50-odd-mile coastline, making 26 stops, at such places as Llwyngwril and Penrhyndeudraeth. But this afternoon there is a side trip of considerable significance at Towyn, to catch the Talyllyn Railway's quaint little train for a ride to Abergynolwyn and Nant Gwernol.

The cult of ancient train worship has spread round the world and is now famous rather than extraordinary, but Towyn is where it all started. The Talyllyn Railway was the first railway to be run successfully by a group of train lovers; it commenced operations nearly 30 years ago. In this way began 'The Great Little Trains of Wales,' of which there are now eight; on this brief excursion we shall travel on two of them.

As the little train puffs up the valley, one's only criticism (and an absurd one) might be that the quaintness of the days when tourists were an afterthought and secondary to the transport of slate, has gone, to be replaced by the efficiency needed to handle 175,000 passenger journeys each summer and to survive in a harsh business world.

Pushing on northwards from Towyn, two hours and 17 stations later we alight at Minffordd for the greatest of the 'Great Little Trains.' On the way we have passed Fairbourne, where the smallest of them is found, and crossed the Mawddach estuary by a great bridge, the longest in Wales. Minffordd is a two-level station and up above are the slim gauge tracks of the famous Festiniog Railway, where some 115 years ago, the concept of narrow-gauge steam railways for general transport was born.

The fact that the Festiniog Railway's annual journey count approaches 400,000, most of them packed (literally) into the summer peak months, means that a little subtlety is required during that period to obtain good seats. That we are one station up from the lower terminus means that trains going up will be full; but we can squeeze into one going down and be already inside when the multitude storms the train at Porthmadog Harbour terminus. Most trains have buffet-cars, first-class accommodation and observation cars and are hauled by oil-fired steam locomotives. The best vantage point to see some lovely scenery is the same side as the platform at Minffordd.

Like the Talyllyn, the Festiniog Railway was built (in 1836) as a tramway to bring slates down from the quarries in the hinterland. Unlike the Talyllyn it was laid out so that gravity could be used to bring loaded trains downhill, horses (which travelled down in 'dandy cars') drawing the empties back up. In 1864 the FR was converted to a steam 'common-carrier' railway but the original dates of construction and incorporation means that the Festiniog Railway Company is the oldest surviving concern in the world's rail transport business, having been operating since 1836 and having been in continuous legal existence since 1832.

In 1954 Alan Pegler of *Flying Scotsman* fame acquired a controlling interest in the line which

The 0–4–2T *Talyllyn* in action on the Talyllyn Railway.

was at the time almost wholly derelict. Since 1954 volunteers and a dedicated band of paid staff have brought it to its present premier position among the pleasure railways of the world.

From Porthmadog the FR crosses a great embankment over what was once an arm of the sea; then, on a constantly rising gradient, the little locomotive (it could be one of the unique 'Fairlie' articulated engines) puts out some wonderful exhaust music as the line climbs higher and higher above the beautiful Vale of Festiniog. At Dduallt the original course is left for a spiral and a new section of railway (including a tunnel), which raises the line above a new reservoir.

The original line is rejoined for a final and fascinating section in and out of the houses of Blaenau in the outskirts of Festiniog to reach (by 1981 or 1982) a new station in the town center. Currently this last mile is served by connecting bus, or can be walked.

At Blaenau Festiniog, a scenic British Rail branch connects the town to the north coast (if one has time to spare, there are some underground 'tram' trips into the mountains to see how slate was won). From there, if one takes the afternoon train, British Rail will bring him back to London's new and handsome Euston station by evening.

Left:
Volunteers hard at work on the restoration of the Festiniog Railway.

Below:
The brand new Fairlie 0–4–4–0T locomotive *Earl of Merioneth* leaves Tan-y-Grisiau station on the newly opened Deviation line of the Festiniog Railway.

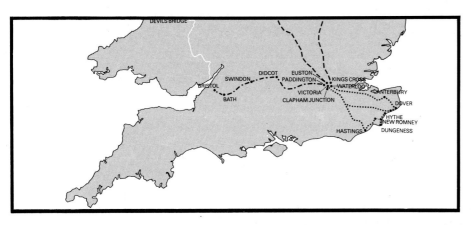

Route 2 God's Wonderful Railway

Our second trip is completed in a single day from London. It begins at Paddington station where, on the 'Lawn' under engineer Isambard Kingdom Brunel's (1806–1859) great roof, a large number of railway fans enjoy the feeling of being on holy ground. The reason is that Paddington is where one of the world's great railway companies, the Great Western Railway, had its beginnings. Incidentally, the 'Lawn' is the name given to the circulating area at the end of the platforms. Here another High Speed Train awaits our patronage.

Brunel himself would certainly have approved of the speed as well as the boldness of the concept of these trains. He would also have been pleased to see, as the train rolls through the London suburbs, that his great viaduct at Hanwell still stands, carrying HSTs and diesel-powered freight-liners just as safely as the little single-driver locomotives of his day. Even more pleasing to him would be the Thames bridge at Maidenhead, the collapse of which the pundits of his day forecast as being imminent. His great brick arches, the flattest of their kind ever built, are still perfect.

The immense cutting at Sonning approaching Reading was another of the great man's achievements and, after brief halts there and at Didcot, Swindon is reached, 63 minutes after leaving Paddington, at 10.48. During the 1930s the GWR ran a steam train – then the fastest booked run in the world – from here to Paddington in 65 minutes, but no stops could be managed on that timing!

There are things to do and see at Swindon. First, a cup of coffee in the station buffet to judge whether things have improved since Brunel wrote his famous letter . . .

Dear Sir, I assure you Mr Player was wrong in

Left:
Brunel's famous Wharn-
cliffe Viaduct at Hanwell,
Middlesex. It was the first
work to be started in making
the Great Western Rail-
way from London to
Bristol; and it is still carrying traffic today.

Above:
A 4–6–0, No 5069 *Isambard
Kingdom Brunel*, brings the
Merchant Venturer express
through Wiltshire.

Extreme left:
The London to Penzance
sleeping car express stands
at No 1 platform at Pad-
dington station and fills
with passengers.

supposing that I thought you purchased inferior coffee. I thought I said to him I was
surprised you should buy such bad roasted
corn. I did not believe you had such a thing as
coffee in the place; I am certain I never tasted
any. I have long since ceased to make com-
plaints at Swindon. I avoid taking anything
there if I can help it.

Yours faithfully,
I K Brunel

Second, the GWR Museum with many treasures lies a short walk (go outside and turn right)
from the station. There are several full-size
locomotives, including a replica 7ft gauge *North
Star* of 1838 and some more modern locomotives,
typical of the brassy, coppery green monsters
that ran on the main line above until 20 years ago.
The Locomotive Factory is nearby (but not
normally open to visitors) and also the carefully
planned Victorian 'company town' for the men

who worked there is all around. Not many of its inhabitants work for the railway now, though.

The best view of the Works is from the railway (on the 'up' or north side) and for this one must wait until the next HST comes along for Bristol – although waiting passengers should see one or two going through 'hitting the ton' in the meantime. A stop is made at Chippenham, then one enters and exits the 1¾-mile Box tunnel which, at such speed, is a mere flicker. At one time stage coaches were run from Chippenham to Bath 'for persons fearful of Box tunnel'! Legend has it that the tunnel is set out on a gradient so that the sun shines through on Brunel's (the builder) birthday. In fact for some reason it is a few days different; the actual date is 21 April, but one needs to be there soon after six o'clock in the morning.

Bath is worth an extended visit not only to take the waters and examine the Roman Baths but to enjoy the superb Georgian architecture of this lovely town. Following Bath Temple Meads station, Bristol is our destination. Nearby is another of Brunel's creations, his iron ship *Great Britain* which recently returned to her home port for restoration. When completed in 1844, she was the largest ship ever built.

Queen Victoria's husband, Prince Albert, launched the *Great Britain* on 19 July 1843; after the ceremony Daniel Gooch, GWR's young locomotive superintendent, personally drove the Prince's special home to London in 124 minutes at an average speed of 57mph!

One of his 'Fire Fly' class single-wheelers would have been used. Early broad-gauge locomotives were all named, and never suffered the indignity of numbers. Imagine tearing through the then-unspoilt countryside on a summer's evening, at the throttle of one of these lovely little fire-chariots (of one's own design, too) and on such an errand.

Brunel's original station at Temple Meads still exists as part of the modern one, though now as a covered parking lot. It is certainly worth a glance, showing how lavish in conception was the original GWR.

On the way back to London, one might choose a train that makes a stop at Didcot to visit the Great Western Society's live museum of steam. Didcot is about an hour's journey from Bristol. Only 20 years ago one might have made this 60-minute Bristol–Didcot run in an amazing vehicle called a 'slip coach,' which was detached from the main train before it passed through the station at speed. The 'slip' was then braked to a stand in the platform. Slip coaches were a GWR speciality which lasted into the 1950s, although they had only a short existence elsewhere.

Didcot has a vast collection of GWR artifacts, including much rolling stock in running order. Full-length steam-hauled trains, formed from material held and restored here, venture out on to British Rail lines on special occasions. In fact, there are over 25 locomotives, 32 carriages and 15 wagons. And so back to Paddington.

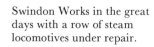

Swindon Works in the great days with a row of steam locomotives under repair.

Route 3
Rush Hour in
the South

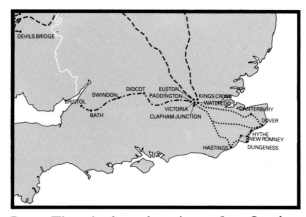

Route Three is also a day trip out from London. This trip begins on the Brighton section of Victoria station (platforms 9–17). Victoria station is a double station, which used to serve the London, Chatham & Dover Railway (the 'Chatham Side') and the London Brighton and South Coast Railway (the 'Brighton Side').

Passengers on this tour should take the first train shown (on the great indicator board) to stop at Clapham Junction. The aim is to see the world's busiest station at its busiest time; between eight and nine o'clock in the morning, something like 250 trains will pass through Clapham Junction, most of them third-rail electric.

Dizziness rather than boredom will indicate when one has had enough and that it is time to catch a Waterloo train, which (again) will depart from the higher-numbered platforms. In this way one can experience crowded train travel as most Londoners know it – but only for a few minutes.

Waterloo is the largest station in Britain and definitely a spectacle at the tail-end of the morning rush-hour. Our aim now is to join the 10 o'clock train from Charing Cross station to Folkestone. It does actually call at Waterloo at 1003 at some curved platforms tucked away out of sight. Railwaymen still know this section of the station as Waterloo Junction, although the actual junction (the connecting line which ran across the main concourse of the main station) was taken out some 65 years ago. To get there, ask for the Charing Cross line platforms; they are across the main carriage road which brings taxis and the like into the station.

If time permits, one can always take the first train back across the river to Charing Cross where the 10 o'clock should be waiting. This train, after its Waterloo stop, runs through commuting country and the 'Stockbroker Belt' to the garden of England, where hops are grown to make Kentish ale. The first stop is Ashford (where

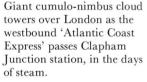

Giant cumulo-nimbus cloud towers over London as the westbound 'Atlantic Coast Express' passes Clapham Junction station, in the days of steam.

British Rail build wagons) and it seems no time at all before one alights at Folkestone, on top of the famous white cliffs.

A double-decker bus or a taxi is necessary to reach the Romney, Hythe & Dymchurch Railway station five miles away at Hythe. A real treat is in store.

In that long ago 'War to end all wars' a prisoner-of-war called Jack Howey had time to reflect on life and what he wanted from it. And what he did when the war was over was to build the largest model railway in the world, 13 miles of double 15in gauge main line laid out on reclaimed land across the famous Romney marshes, on which miniature steam locomotives, one-third full size, still haul over 300,000 passengers each year. The whole railway from locomotives to lavatories was designed by that grand old man of the miniature railway, the late Henry Greenly.

The Dymchurch, New Romney and Dungeness Buffet Car Express drawn up under the roof of Hythe Station is quite a train. At the head stands one of the Romney's superbly groomed 4–6–2s – perhaps *Green Goddess* or *Southern Maid* – followed by twelve carriages. The buffet car *Courage Belle* is a miracle of ingenuity for a vehicle limited to 3ft 6in in width and 5ft 6in in height. The illusion of a busy railway of the 1920s or 1930s is almost complete. The headquarters of the system with repair shops, locomotive depot, museum, model railway and cafe, is at New Romney – there is also the Captain Howey public house across the road. A frequent daily service runs from April to October and there is the possibility of travelling at week-ends, on the daily schoolchildren's train or a 'Special' outside these months.

If you can manage to look away from the bits of jewelry that the RH & D calls locomotives, many relics of past history are found hereabouts. Nearby are the forts called Martello towers which were built in case Napoleon tried to invade and the first radar station on the hills above the marsh which deterred Hitler from trying it. The place where the Normans defeated the English in 1066 is not far away and could be taken in on the way home. Take a taxi from New Romney to Appledore station and change at Hastings; the station is called Battle and is a few miles from Hastings on the main London line. Instead of visiting Battle one can return to Folkestone and travel via Dover to Canterbury for a look at the Cathedral. Either way British Rail's train service in this part of the United Kingdom is reasonably frequent and reliable.

Below:
Rebuilt 'West Country' class 4–6–2 *Lyme Regis* prepares to leave Waterloo station with one of the last steam express trains to leave the station.

Bottom:
The Romney Hythe & Dymchurch Railway's 4–8–2 *Hercules* in the twilight.

North America

PRINCE RUPERT
PRINCE GEORGE
VANCOUVER

YELLOWHEAD PASS
EDMONTON
KICKING HORSE PASS

CANADA
CHURCHILL
HUDSON BAY
WINNIPEG
OBA

UNITED STATES

OGDEN
CHEYENNE
CHICAGO
MONTREAL
TORONTO
NIAGRA FALLS
SYDNEY
HALIFAX

SAN FRANCISCO
OAKLAND
SAN JOSE
GRAND CANYON
LOS ANGELES
FLAGSTAFF
SILVERTON
DURANGO
CHAMA
DENVER
ANTONITO
ALBUQUERQUE
KANSAS CITY
CHATTANOOGA
ATLANTA
NEW YORK
WASHINGTON
ORLANDO

MEXICO

0   SCALE   500 MILES

Perhaps the nicest thought about travelling by train in the United States of America is that, when you put the dollars for your fare down on the counter, kind Uncle Sam stands beside you and adds a similar sum as his contribution. The reason is that Amtrak, formerly called the National Rail Passenger Corporation, which has, since 1970, run most of the nation's passenger trains – other than commuter or suburban trips – does so under a Federal Government subsidy of over 100 percent of receipts.

Compared with the great trains of yesteryear, Amtrak's service is a trifle homespun and there are still reliability problems to solve. In a world where rail speeds elsewhere are increasing by leaps and bounds, Amtrak has often tended to get slower. For example, it is not always able to offer long-distance transit times which even approach those achieved with steam in the 1930s, let alone early diesel timings of the 1950s.

One answer is, perhaps, that there is no point in so doing. When the journey between Chicago and Los Angeles (city center to city center) takes five hours by air and 46 hours by rail, perhaps it is better for Amtrak to concentrate on clients to whom time is not important. Only 30,000 out of 200,000 miles of railroad in the USA (by far the smallest proportion of any major country) have passenger service but, even so, service is provided between a good many important cities. Long-distance trains have dining or buffet cars and, if overnight, sleeping accommodation as well as sit-up coaches.

A good buy for visitors is Amtrak's USA rail-pass, valid for 14, 21 or 30 days. It does, however, have two quite serious drawbacks. First, sleeper reservations, the cost of which of course are not included in the price, cannot be made by pass-holders until one hour before the train departs. Second, you cannot just hop on a train – you have to obtain a separate ticket prior to *each* journey from the ticket office.

The larger though much less populous 'half' of North America is called Canada and has nearly as much passenger railroad as its southern neighbor. VIA Rail Canada is responsible for almost all passenger reservations and journeys by rail in Canada. Passenger rail services in Canada, as in the United States, have declined in the last few years, but VIA Rail still runs several 'near-de-luxe' transcontinental trains – these will be discussed in Route 6.

Atchison, Topeka & Santa Fe Railroad's eastbound 'Super Chief' threads Apache Canyon near Lamy, New Mexico.

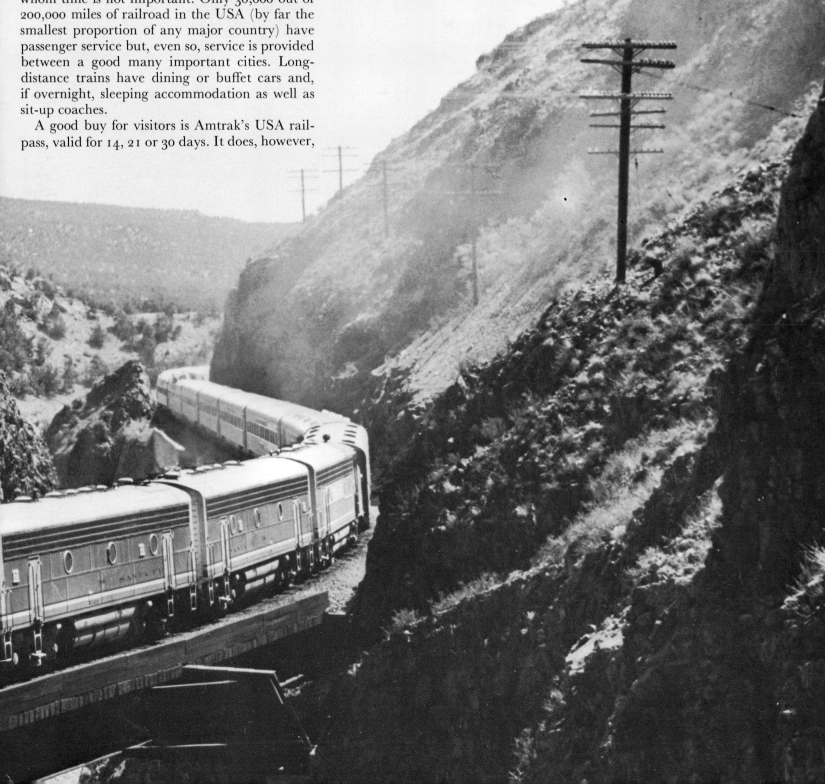

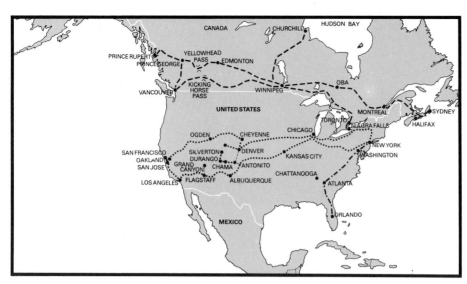

Route 4 Overland Routes

Capturing all the world's imagination are the great transcontinental coast-to-coast expresses of the USA and no world train traveller worthy of the name could possibly omit such an excursion from his itinerary. The only problem is that they do not exist and never have done! Of course, one can split hairs and call the train on the 56-mile railroad across the Isthmus of Panama a transcontinental, but for serious coast-to-coast travellers there have been, at best and occasionally, dubious through cars by various routes. With these very limited exceptions, it has always been a case of 'change at Chicago or St Louis or New Orleans,' with the *sotto voce* lament, 'A hog can cross America without changing trains, but *you* can't.'

Nevertheless New York seems the obvious place to start and San Francisco the place to end a first journey in North America.

In those heady days of 15 years ago, it was still just possible for a traveller to begin going west, as far as Chicago, on the most famous train in the world, the 'Twentieth Century Limited'; but if Amtrak's substitute 'Lake Shore Limited' does not match up to the 'Century''s style, at least it does offer a sleeping and dining car service to Chicago by this route. It must be admitted that the journey now takes 20 hours 40 minutes,

compared with the 15½ hours achieved thirty years ago.

Still, it was a lifelong ambition fulfilled to enter the great hall of New York City's Grand Central station, a ticket for the 'Century' in one's pocket, tread that flamboyant (if a trifle frayed) red carpet on the platform at Track 34 and climb aboard.

It was also a dream come true to sip a drink in the observation car, as the famous four-track main line of the New York Central coiled away behind, with the Hudson River alongside. Dinner in the diner was good rather than memorable – and an introduction to that excellent US custom of writing out your own bill. The diesels up ahead forged on tirelessly through the night, while one Englishman aboard slept away jet lag in that peculiar American convenience, the railroad roomette. It was confirmation of a long-suspected fact that longitudinal berths (general practise in the USA) were more comfortable than transverse ones (as in Europe).

The days are long past when there were both fresh- and salt-water baths available on board to wash away the grime of the journey or when the President of the New York Central Railroad would have a list of travelling VIPs and the actual arrival time of the 'Century' as the top item of correspondence on his desk when he got to the office each morning. But even so, riding the 'Century' was a great experience even in its declining years.

Having left Chicago, the 'Windy City,' one could (and still can) travel for a whole day behind a big North American steam locomotive. The Chicago, Burlington and Quincy's oil-fired 4–8–4

Above:
The observation car of the 'Twentieth Century Limited' before departure from Chicago.

Extreme left:
The New York Central Railroad's 'Twentieth Century Limited' at speed along the Hudson River.

No 5632 did the honors for the author all the next day. The trail led from Chicago to Galesburg, Illinois, mostly via devious Burlington branch lines, on which the famous US run-past technique was staged (unbelievably it was also done on the main line). Run-pasts are an attempt to solve the tiresome paradox that, if one travels in a train, one cannot photograph it or see it. They are done in the following manner. The train stops, its occupants get out, the train backs up a mile and returns, driven all-out with the oil turned up to give lots of lovely exhaust music and clouds of black smoke. Photos are taken, the train stops way out beyond, backs up again, the passengers get in and the train continues on its route. It is the kind of thing that is absolute anathema to the rail authorities in the author's own country and in many others. Incidentally, although No 5632 no longer performs for her fans, several other big North American steamers do.

The trip above was part and parcel of an affair which was at that time an annual event, the Illini Railroad Club's excursion to Colorado, under the genial leadership of Maurice Klebolt. At Lincoln, the party had accommodation reserved on the 'Denver Zephyr' train and soon enough was rolling across the prairies, apparently flat but in fact gently ascending to the mile-high city (Denver's altitude is 5280ft). Next morning the sleepers were worked to Colorado Springs and from there it was an all-day bus ride through Colorado, the 'Garden of the Gods,' to a place whose very name stirs the blood of any rail fan . . . Alamosa, gateway to the narrow gauge.

The predecessors of that smart modern railroad, the Denver & Rio Grande Western – Rio Grande for short – covered the mountains of Colorado and New Mexico with a maze of narrow (3ft) gauge lines. Abandonment and conversion to standard gauge had by 1960 reduced them to two remnants – a 250-mile line from Alamosa to Durango and Farmington, and another branch from Durango to Silverton, around 300 miles in

all. In 1964 the Rio Grande – on this totally steam-operated line – was operating two freights a week and two excursions a year out of Alamosa; the author was on one of them.

The reason for this excitement was manifold. The D & RGW narrow-gauge lines were then the last surviving one-thousandth of North American big-time steam railroading. Furthermore, they maintained all usual fixings such as trestles, wyes, balloon loops and snow-sheds, four percent grades, timber-lined tunnels, rotary steam snow-plows, gons, reefers, stock cars, cabooses, as well as the Baldwin and Alco 2–8–2s. There was 'Injun Country' (although the Navajo never caused the problems over the white take-over that tribes like the Apaches and the Sioux did), canyons, 10,000ft summits, sage-brush desert and all the rest – so familiar the world over from the dozens of movies made there.

Movies, however, are not as impressive as the real thing; they do not offer the scent of coal smoke amongst the Colorado pines. Neither are they shown in cinemas which are air-conditioned with real Colorado mountain air, like the open observation car on our little train. Today the most spectacular part of this railroad, the 67 miles from Antonito to Chama, is operated twice a week in each direction. This Cumbres and Toltec Scenic Railroad, as it is called, is Number 1 both in length and in scenery amongst the tourist railways of the world.

Chicago, Burlington & Quincy Railroad's oil-fired 4–8–4 No 5632 hauls a steam special for enthusiasts from Chicago, Illinois to Lincoln, Nebraska.

Above:
Denver & Rio Grande
2–8–2 No 478

Right:
A ten-car BART (Bay Area Rapid Transit) train passes through a residential section of Union City in southern Alameda County. The train is as long as the Bank of America building in San Francisco is tall, carries 720 seated passengers, and during morning and evening commuter hours can accommodate 1440 passengers.

Number 2 is Colorado's famous Silverton Train out of Durango, run for so long by the big-time railroad, Denver & Rio Grande Western. The operation was sold to a private firm at the end of the 1979 season. After steaming for several hours up the Canyon of the River of Lost Souls, with rocky cliffs and 10,000ft peaks above, one finally arrives at Silverton where one is treated to a mock gun-fight and finds good ladies masquerading as saloon hostesses, all by courtesy of the enterprising inhabitants of what would otherwise be a ghost town.

From Denver, reached then as now by more prosaic means of transport, the next objective was San Francisco. The 'San Francisco Zephyr' goes all the way to the San Francisco Bay, over the original Union Pacific-Southern (Central) Pacific transcontinental route via Ogden. A possible side-trip while at Denver is a ride to Grand Junction and back on the non-Amtrak 'Rio Grande Zephyr' which goes 'through the Rockies not around them' (as the D & RGW's slogan

states). Fifteen years ago the corresponding trains were the 'City of San Francisco' and the 'California Zephyr,' the latter going right through to Oakland via Ogden and the Feather River Canyon on the Western Pacific. Incidentally, Union Pacific has kept its last steam locomotive, 4-8-4 No 8444, maintained in running order and based near Denver.

It is sad that the 23-mile crossing of the Great Salt Lake near Ogden, once the longest railway bridge in the world but now a rock fill, takes place in the middle of the night. Breakfast time finds one in Reno, Nevada, then comes the famous crossing of the Sierra at Emigrant Gap and the long run down (so welcome in covered-wagon days) into California. San Francisco Bay (or the arm of it that becomes the Sacramento River) is crossed by the bridge over the Straits of Carquinez.

No longer does the Southern Pacific take you down to the station on the mole at Oakland, nor do SP steamers ferry one across the bay. Even BART, the new rapid-transit system in the

Above:
The beautiful Wasatch Mountains form a striking background for 4-8-4 No 8444 as it hauls a Union Pacific Rocky Mountain Railroad Club special around a curve at Roy.

Top:
A few miles east of Green River, Wyoming, Union Pacific's eastbound 'City of Los Angeles' makes its way across the continent on the original Overland Route.

Above:
The end of an era – a vestigial diesel-hauled express train in the last days of Southern Pacific long-distance passenger service.

Top:
A San Francisco cable car on the turntable at the junction of Bay and Taylor Streets.

Right:
Several railroads in North America, including Canadian Pacific, Burlington Northern and Southern Pacific use these unusual high-capacity double-deck passenger cars for commuter services.

Extreme right:
Denver & Rio Grande Western Railroad's 'Rio Grande Zephyr' express approaches the east portal of the Moffat Tunnel.

Bay Area, is not very convenient, so it is a case of catching a connecting bus across the famous Bay Bridge to San Francisco. [This receding of railroads from great but costly stations is much easier to bring about in North America than in Britain, because the US absence of need for raised (and very permanent) platforms means that any track with a space alongside it will do as a substitute.]

San Francisco's best-known attraction is a rail-borne one; a ride on the famous cable-cars should on no account be missed. The thrills are at least double the expectation. The procedures at junctions and cable crossings are heroic and any admirer of ingenious contraptions and contrivances is in his element at the central winding house (at Mason and Washington), whence cables go snaking around under the streets all over a large section of the city. The amount of hidden hardware challenges the imagination even now, when only three lines, one-tenth of the original network of 50 miles, are in operation.

Another recommended day out from San Francisco for rail enthusiasts is to Tilden Regional Park above Berkeley, where the delightful 15in gauge Redwood Valley Railroad adjoins the new $7\frac{1}{2}$in and $4\frac{3}{4}$in gauge tracks of the Golden Gate Live Steamers (operational at week-ends). The Redwood Valley is a miniature version, of a narrow-gauge 'Wild West' railway, while the Live Steamers' track is a kind of 'Land Where The Old Engines Go.' Here little one-twelfth and one-eighth scale locomotives, with real fire in their bellies, recreate the lost world of steam, hauling their owners and builders as well as friends.

Back in San Francisco, one can even dine out in rail-fan style, at the Victoria Station Restaurant.

The 'Coast Starlight' express to Los Angeles leaves from Oakland. This may seem an odd title for a train which makes the run in day-time – but in fact it started back in Seattle the previous day. One can catch it at San José after an 80-minute 47-mile trip on Southern Pacific's only peninsular commuter passenger service. Two things should be noted as one climbs aboard a double-decker coach at SP's 'Third and Townsend' station: first, the express train's noble predecessor, the 'Coast Daylight' began its run at this station and, second, SP found this suburban operation such a burden that the company recently offered to set up its regular riders with free mini-buses, if SP was, in return, allowed to discontinue the service. Even though this offer was not taken up, one should check the timetable first – reflecting that this pathetic little square of paper is all that remains of one of the finest passenger train programs ever offered to the public in any country.

The oil-fired 'Daylight' streamlined 4–8–4s of the late 1930s would have made mincemeat of Amtrak's present-day diesel schedule, but it is still a fine ride – often in sight of the Pacific Ocean – via San Luis Obispo and Santa Barbara to the 'City of the Angels.' A dome car is now provided for observation on the 10-hour 50-minute run

Right:
Atchison, Topeka & Santa Fe Railway's streamlined diesel locomotive for the 'Super Chief' train is cleaned in an automatic washing plant.

Extreme right:
Amtrak's discontinued 'National Limited' express from Kansas City to New York.

and this is perhaps some compensation for the 1-hour 20-minute slowing which has taken place over the last 40 years. However, nothing will ever compensate for the loss of those lovely orange and black steam locomotives, although a restored one had a coast-to-coast outing recently in connection with the US bi-centenary celebrations. But neither Southern Pacific nor Santa Fe are normally steam nostalgia lines.

Los Angeles has a superb Spanish-style station with many platforms to serve today's meagre eight daily pairs of trains. Forty years ago the whole area was served by a vast network of local electric railroads but nowadays the only practicable method of transport for tourists in Los Angeles is an automobile and in this way one can see, according to taste, such delights as the Homes of the Stars, the *Queen Mary* liner, movie studios, Forest Lawn Cemetery and (with a railway flavor) Knott's Berry Farm and Disneyland.

Now the tourist is free to head north to Arizona using Atchison, Topeka and Santa Fe tracks but nowadays on Amtrak's 'South West Limited' rather than Santa Fe's 'Super Chief.' Two comments are worthy of note: first, what befell Gene Wilder when making this trip on a film train called 'Silver Streak' (run by a mysterious organization called 'Amroad' – whose train, incidentally, bore a strange resemblance to Canadian Pacific's) need not be feared and, second, the legendary traditions of service laid down by Santa Fe influence Amtrak's staff to keep up theirs. Incidentally, Santa Fe's catering was from the earliest days, for the West, of un-heard-of quality. England-born Fred Harvey was responsible; he obtained the catering concession from the Santa Fe in 1860. Not only were his food and his restaurants respectable but also his

waitresses. Elsewhere, the ladies who served in the eating houses of the West had a certain well-deserved reputation. The Harvey girls' respectability was, however, not at the expense of their charm because among the good things that Fred Harvey offered his customers should be included the thousands of his girls who married and settled in Santa Fe territory.

Dinner in the diner is the first thing to discuss whether, as in the past, on 'Super Chief' or as in the present, on the 'South West Limited.' One arrives in Arizona the next morning, running on one of the few lines in the USA which boast European railway speeds. The Grand Canyon is only 60 miles to the north; Santa Fe has a branch to the Grand Canyon from Winslow and for many years sleeping cars were detached from the 'Grand Canyon Limited' to spend a day's stopover there. There is talk of running this branch as a steam tourist railway but, in the meantime, the recommendation is that today's tourist rent a car at Flagstaff to visit one of the greatest spectacles in the world and then book a mule – mule-back is the only means of transport down into the canyon.

When the writer rode the 'Super Chief' he could not resist the thought of a second helping of Rio Grande. Durango is only 100 miles to the north, a little further to the east. However, one must fly or take a car or bus from the Grand Canyon to Durango as the journey by rail has not been possible since 1939, when the Denver & Rio Grande closed its narrow-gauge line from Antonito to Santa Fe (and, incidentally, lost thereby all justification to its namesake).

To return to New York, one can rejoin the 'South West Limited' for Chicago at Albuquerque and then join the 'Broadway Limited' via Pittsburg, the Horseshoe Curve and Philadelphia.

Route 5
No
Choo-Choos to
Chattanooga

CHATTANOOGA

'You leave the Pennsylvania station at a
  quarter-to-four
Read a magazine and then you're in
  Baltimore
Dinner in the diner, nothing could be finer
Than to have your ham-and-eggs in Carolina'

For several reasons it is no longer possible to have
'dinner in the diner' – or, for that matter, 'ham
and eggs in Carolina' on a 'Chattanooga Choo-
Choo.' In the first place, there are no express
passenger trains from New York (or, indeed,
anywhere) to Chattanooga; secondly, if there
were they would have diesels not 'choo-choos' on
the front; thirdly, one would not go via Carolina,
as the line passes directly from Virginia into
Tennessee and always has. Apart from these
trifles, it's an excellent account and of course,
Carolina rhymes so nicely with diner! Thirty
years ago, incidentally, two trains made the trip
daily, neither of them leaving the Pennsylvania
station at a quarter to four, but at either 12.30 pm
(the 'Southerner') or 6.50 pm (the 'Pelican').
Best forget about the 'Tennessean' which departed at 3.30 am – but berths were available
from 11 pm.

The nearest convenient place to Chattanooga
which can be reached from New York is Atlanta,
Georgia, and one can travel to it today leaving
Pennsylvania station at a quarter to *three*, on the
electrified main line to Washington, Amtrak's
own piece of railroad. Baltimore is reached at
1755 (so, if one wants to follow the words of the
song, it would have to be a very absorbing and
verbose magazine). However, one of the best
diners in the USA comes on at Washington.
Until very recently this was worked by one of the
very few non-Amtrak passenger operators, Southern Railway. Since the 'Crescent' is scheduled
to cross the state line leaving Carolina well before
dawn, one would have to settle for ham-and-eggs

in Georgia, before arriving in Atlanta at 8.40 in the morning.

Southern Railway is also one of those few railroad companies which run steam locomotives for pleasure trips and some of these happenings take place out of Chattanooga and Atlanta, usually on weekends. Others start from Alexandria, Virginia, not far from Washington. Thus it might still be that a real 'choo-choo' could be going the 153 miles north by northwest from Atlanta to Chattanooga, but otherwise it would have to be the bus. . . . [Incidentally, this line is not the setting of that famous incident in the Civil War when Union troops stole the locomotive *General*, only to be chased and captured by the Confederates in the *Texas*; that particular line also goes from Atlanta to Chattanooga but now belongs to Seaboard Coast Line. The *General* has survived and, being in working order, is occasionally run.]

Three days a week the 'Crescent' goes on from Atlanta to New Orleans. A sleeping car is passed on to the 'Sunset Limited' for Los Angeles; during the overnight stop-over, the car can be used as a hotel. Four nights are spent on board during the coast-to-coast ride. This route (in the reverse direction) could have been used in place of that via Santa Fe and the Grand Canyon, described previously (Route 4) but, in the writer's case, it would have precluded that double-portion of wonderful Denver & Rio Grande in Colorado.

Ian Fleming's train 'Silver Phantom' in his James Bond novel *Live and Let Die* is a thinly disguised version of Seaboard Coast Line's 'Silver Star'; Amtrak still runs the train to much the same schedule. [In fact, Fleming wrote his account first-hand from journeys he often made en route to his home in Jamaica, but he usually started from Washington. It never occurred to him that the great diesels marked 'Seaboard Air Line' would not have come on at New York, but he did spot that a few of the cars would be lettered 'Richmond, Fredericksburg & Potomac' for the short but busy line that acted as a 'bridge road' between the once mighty Pennsylvania Railroad (now part of Conrail) and the Seaboard Air Line.]

One of the stops along the route allows passengers to disembark and enjoy Florida's Disney World at Orlando. At Disney World the formula that made Disneyland, California such a success, has been applied on a much larger scale. Of course, this formula includes small steam railroads of superb concept but of unrealistically manicured quality; the two at Disney World are called the 'Magic Kingdom' and the 'Wilderness' Railroads. Having enjoyed all the fanciful and entertaining components of Disney World, one can board 'Silver Star' or its companion 'Silver Meteor' to return to reality once again.

Left:
Florida East Coast Railway's northbound 'Champion' express from Miami to Chicago at Hale Sound, Florida.

Below:
Seaboard Air Line's 'Silver Meteor' express near Sebring, Florida.

Route 6
Polar Bears and Kicking Horses

Although having only one-tenth the population, Canada operates nearly as much passenger railway as the United States. Until 1978 there were two main operators – privately owned Canadian Pacific and publicly owned Canadian National – but now the passenger trains on these lines are run by one Crown corporation, VIA Rail Canada. A feature (very welcome once it begins to work) is to be a computerized reservation system integrated with that of the national airline, Air Canada, whereby one can make – for the first time in the recent history of travel – train and airline bookings at one time, together with car rental and hotels reservations.

If you count the tide-waters of the St Lawrence River at Montreal as the ocean then the 'Super-Continental' is a true transcontinental service. The 2915-mile journey to Vancouver is certainly the longest possible North American journey one can take in one train. Pedants who believe the ocean begins at the mouth of the St Lawrence can start back at Halifax, Nova Scotia and take the 'Ocean' or 'Scotian' trains to Montreal to join the 'Super-Continental.' Super-pedants can travel further east from Halifax to the eastern-most point to which trains run in North America,

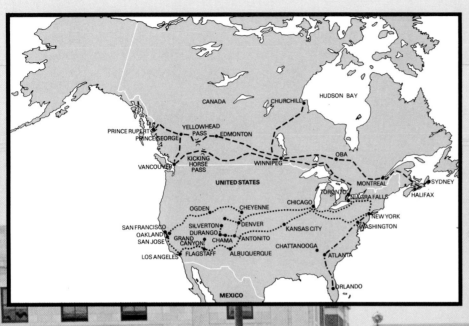

Sydney, Nova Scotia. An added bonus at Sydney during the summer months is the Cape Breton Steam Railway which has a British 'Schools' class 4–4–0. A through sleeping car runs from Sydney to Montreal, having been attached to the 'Scotian' at Truro, Nova Scotia.

A 'Super-Continental' leaves Montreal each morning but, for reasons explained later, Thursday is our choice.

At North Bay in northern Ontario, reached early the first evening, one might look out for an independent Canadian railway, the Ontario Northland, although its 'Northlander' train, made up of an ex-Trans-Europ-Express diesel set, would not be around at this hour. Rail enthusiasts might look out again in the small hours when the 'Super-Continental' encounters another of the four independent Canadian passenger-hauling roads, the Algoma Central at Oba. This line runs a dining-car train six times a week south to the Great Lakes. Rides on both these lines – 600 miles northward on the ONR by 'Polar Bear' express to Moosonee and 250 miles southward on ACR – are possibilities; both provide meal service and are the only land transport of any kind in much of the area they serve.

The 'Super-Continental' reaches Winnipeg, the capital city of Manitoba and the gateway to the prairies, in the late evening of the second day. From Winnipeg the journey could simply continue on the 'Super-Continental' but the suggestion is that one should drop off and stay the night and then do the side-trip to end all side-trips by taking 'Train 93' to the port of Churchill on Hudson Bay, 999 miles and two nights and a day to the north. 'Train 93' runs on Sundays, Tuesdays and Thursdays, departing in the afternoon. Three things might draw one to Churchill – first, it is one of those journeys that, once accomplished, would certainly put a rail traveller into the elite class. Second, mixed freight and passenger trains are all too rare nowadays, but a mixed train with diner and sleeper is *la crème de la crème*. Third, if Uncle Sam stands beside each passenger at Amtrak's ticket windows and matches him dollar for dollar then at Winnipeg, when one asks for a ticket to Churchill, the Canadian government vicariously adds nine dollars to each one of the passenger's to cover the cost of the ride.

Earlier in this volume (page 12) the author outlined the necessary conditions for a train to be classed de-luxe. It must be noted that no one

A 1930s Canadian National Railway's station scene at Hamilton, Ontario.

By breakfast time the '93' is at Le Pas, a vastly remote junction in Manitoba. Soon afterwards it enters the no-man's land of northern Manitoba. There are difficulties with track maintenance in these barren wastes, because they are usually-but-not-quite-always frozen and this is reflected in our 25mph rate of progress. The trip out and back to Churchill takes four nights and three days, with most of one day available for sightseeing in this remote seaside resort. In the summer, one can see grain being loaded into ships; spring and autumn is notable for an infestation of polar bears – Churchill was sited on one of their migratory routes. At this juncture one could fly back to Winnipeg in two hours or as a dedicated rail traveller take the train again and arrive back in Winnipeg on Thursday at 0800 hours.

It should be noted that if one happened to be in Winnipeg on a summer Sunday there is the Prairie Dog Central Steam Vintage Railway to see. A veteran Rogers 4–4–0, of the type that built Canada, runs out of Winnipeg at 12 noon for a two-hour 36-mile round trip. Tickets and information are available from the Vintage Locomotive Society, Incorporated, Box 1182, Winnipeg, Manitoba, Canada.

As the timetable is at present, the train from Churchill leaves one with most of the day to spend in Winnipeg before taking another west-bound 'Super-Continental' – seven complete sets are needed to provide daily service. During its 60-minute stop, the modest train that left Mont-

Above:
Up-to-the-minute transport – a Canadian National Turbo-train leaves Montreal.

Top:
Canadian Pacific's 'Canadian' transcontinental express crosses Stoney Creek Bridge, British Columbia.

thought to add a stipulation saying that no freight cars were to be attached nor, indeed, specifying a limit to the number of stops – in fact, 'Train 93' makes 93 stops which can hardly be a coincidence. Actually, only the two day coaches in 93's consist rob her of the de-luxe accolade, because the diner does both *table d'hôte* and *à la carte* and one of the two sleepers has a small lounge for socializing. So, with box cars, reefers (refrigerator cars) and container flats between us and the two locomotive units, this incredible mixed nearly-de-luxe train sets out for the northern wilderness.

CP's eastbound Canadian transcontinental express enters the spiral tunnel on the ascent of the Kicking Horse Pass.

real 1½ days earlier, is made up at Winnipeg to (typically) 18 cars – two baggage vans, three coaches, eight sleepers, two 'day-niter' (!) coaches, one super-dome-observation car and two restaurant cars (one serving snacks). Pulled by three diesel units this immense train rolls on through the famous wheatlands; 4 pm the next day finds the traveller in Edmonton, Alberta, with watches set to Mountain Time. Canadian National Railways' crossing of the Rockies is by the relatively easily graded Yellowhead Pass; before crossing the pass, however, there is an historically important diversion to make on a line which was originally the modestly entitled Grand Trunk Pacific and whose objective was not Vancouver but an excellent deep-water port called Prince Rupert further north and actually on the Pacific.

To reach Prince Rupert, one must descend from the 'Super-Continental' in late evening at the mountain resort of Jasper. (One can, of course, continue on the 'Super-Continental' all the way to Vancouver.) An hour after leaving the 'Super-Continental' (just enough time to inspect the preserved CN steam 4–8–2 at Jasper station), one should catch Train No 9. A greater contrast could not be imagined: No 9 has five cars – one baggage, one lounge-diner, two coaches and a single sleeper. At Red Pass Junction, just beyond Yellowhead, she diverts (by going straight ahead) from the 'Super-Continental''s course. Although a lot of the ride is in darkness, the Sunday evening arrival at Prince Rupert allows a view of some

fierce Rocky Mountain bridging and grading over the last 450 miles or so. We are now 4135 direct rail miles (6133 the way we went) from Sydney, Nova Scotia and due for a night in an hotel.

To get to Vancouver from Prince Rupert there are air services, occasional steamers and a train connection involving yet another company, the British Columbia Railway. To travel by train, one should take 'No 9''s opposite, 'No 10,' and retrace one's steps 470 miles to Prince George where there is (provided one has spent an extra night in Jasper) a connection early the next morning on BCR's Tuesday, Thursday and Saturday only 'Cariboo Dayliner' buffet-equipped railcar to Vancouver.

Although one should check ahead in case of changes, one is now poised for one of the world's finest steam-for-pleasure rides. The British Columbia Government has restored one of Canada's most famous locomotives, a Montreal-built Canadian Pacific 'Royal Hudson' 4–6–4, and it is run from Wednesday to Sunday each week in the summer, on a day out among 'Beautiful BC''s best scenery, over the metals of the BCR. Any stop-over in Vancouver should include this experience – a definite must for all rail buffs.

Now it is time to head back across Canada, this time on a train that in Canadian Pacific days was outstanding in the world – the 'Canadian.' Before 1978 the Canrailpass covered only Canadian National rail journeys; journeys on Canadian

The restored Canadian Pacific *Royal Hudson* 4–6–4 No 2860 on its regular tourist working between Vancouver and Squamish in British Columbia.

Pacific trains needed to be paid for separately and the rates were 50 percent higher than CN's. It is understood that VIA Rail has changed that, but it remains to be seen whether CP's standards can be maintained.

Up until now it has been implied that the route has been covered in summer – although the autumn is thought by many to be the best season to cross Canada. Spring can be rather terrible and dubious operationally, with snow-slides liable to interrupt rail service. This leaves winter which should not be dismissed, although there are no steam fixes, only (hopefully) steam heat.

Returning in November 1971 from a business trip to the west coast of the USA, the writer, weary of air travel, asked Canadian Pacific in San Francisco what they could do. They instantly flew him and a colleague by CP Air to Vancouver and put the 10-car 'Canadian' virtually at their disposal. This was just before the long Canadian Pacific sea-going tradition (remember, their *Empress* liners were amongst the best that sailed the seas), of including all meals on the price of the ticket, came to an end. It follows that everyone on board turned up for meals – and the 64 seat diner was never as much as half full! In fact, the number-one hazard of the journey was over-eating; it is very hard to send delicious already-paid-for food back to the kitchen.

The famous climb up through the spiral tunnels to the Connaught Tunnel, which takes the Canadian Pacific over the Divide well below the original Kicking Horse Pass line (now the Trans-Canada Highway), is arranged to be enjoyed in daylight. It is specially nice under snow and sun-shine even if just a tear or two has to be shed for the days when the 'Canadian''s predecessor the 'Dominion' came up this great ascent each day, often in several sections, behind two great ten-coupled 'Selkirk' steam locomotives. CP runs its own luxury hotel at Banff, a must if one has the time and has made reservations.

The prairies are rather dreary in winter, as well as being incredibly cold. However, the steam heating systems of the train are meant to last and will keep all passengers free of frostbite for the duration of their journeys.

At Winnipeg in both directions, the 'Canadian' and the 'Super-Continental' exchange cars, so that either route across the Rockies is served by both Montreal and Toronto cars. The Canadian Pacific route east of Winnipeg runs along the north shore of Lake Superior and is ruggedly scenic – in fact, the cost of construction here almost bankrupted the original company. The situation was saved in the nick of time by an up-rising against the Government, who found the unfinished railroad useful for moving troops to the scene; accordingly they were persuaded to come up with some timely extra finance.

The next day brings us to Toronto in the late afternoon, where there is a possibility of occasional steam excursions behind Canadian National's restored 4–8–2 No 6020, a fitting climax to an incredible holiday on rails.

Continental Europe

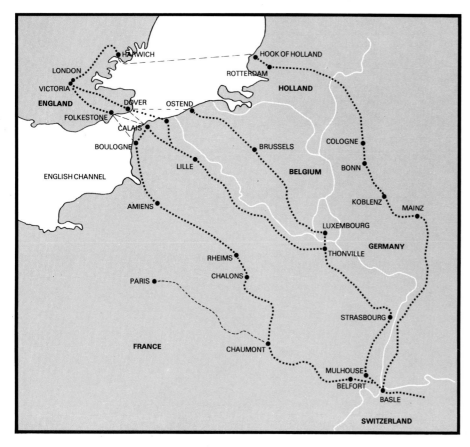

Route 7
Crocodiles
and Christies

Top:
British Rail's 'Golden Arrow' Pullman Car Continental Express passes Hildenborough, Kent on its journey from Dover to London (Victoria), hauled by Class 7 4–6–2 No 70004 *William Shakespeare*.

Extreme right:
The French section of the 'Golden Arrow' Pullman Car Express on the quay at Calais Maritime Station before 1939. The Southern Railway's TS *Canterbury* lies alongside.

European rail travel today has *de jure* only two classes, first and second; but in each of them sleeping car, lie-down (couchette) and ordinary accommodation (seats) are available. This means that *de facto* there are six classes of accommodation. Many trains provide all six! Sleeping cars·are distinguished from couchettes by having made-up beds and a wash-basin. First-class compartments are usually one- or two-berth; second-class three-berth. Couchettes are bunks with a blanket and pillow. In first-class couchettes there are four in each compartment; in second, six. For non-Europeans, a Eur-railpass is available for un-limited period travel; other groups, such as students, can also obtain concessions.

It was in the late 1920s that the author's parents first took him, then still aged under 10, with them on their annual skiing pilgrimages. After the Kaiser's war, strange documents called passports were needed, ever more dubious paper money had replaced gold, but train services on the main Anglo-Swiss route had reached a peak. In those high and far off days the 2 o'clock 'Continental Express' drawn up at Victoria was a train indeed. At its head would be steam (*Sir Francis Drake* or *Sir Walter Raleigh*, perhaps) and a Pullman after-noon tea would be served on the way down to the coast. Passengers would step ashore in France three hours and ten minutes after leaving London. Forty years later British Rail, even with the aid of electric traction, needs four hours to do the job and adds insult to injury by providing elderly and rather undistinguished rolling stock for this LST (Low Speed Train) service.

On the French side of the Channel services are almost as bad. The Anglo-Swiss 'Train CB,'

departing from Calais at 2000, has really very few facilities – no sleeping car (except on a few days around Christmas) and no refreshment car of any kind. Perhaps it says enough that this train runs via Lille and the steel-making towns, while its predecessor went via Rheims and champagne country.

With the present longer route in mind, there-fore, it is perhaps a little unfair to compare the steam running time of nine hours ten minutes, from Calais to Basle with the present electric one which is 30 minutes longer . . . but then French steam locomotives had no rivals for efficiency and performance, even if to young English eyes they had everything but the kitchen sink attached to their complex exteriors. Jokes about their squeaky whistles have turned a little sour when one has since realized that many of them could out-perform anything built anywhere in the world at that time.

It was also somewhat of a shock to see that every French four-wheel box van carried the famous (infamous?) legend '*Hommes 40 – Chevaux 8.*' Not everyone travelled in wagons-lit comfort.

Forty years ago the Swiss train would have consisted of a diner, a baggage car or fourgon

and otherwise only those magnificent blue steel sleeping cars, for Austria, Czechoslovakia, Germany, Hungary, Rumania, as well as the winter sports places.

It was a delightful conceit that each individual sleeping car (or *couplage*, as the case may be) was a separate 'express,' *viz* 'Orient Express' or 'Arlberg-Orient Express' for Bucharest (according to the day of the week), the 'Karlovy Vary Express' for Carlsbad, 'Tyrol Express' for St Auton, Kitzbuhel, 'Engadine Express' for Davos, St Moritz, 'Oberland Express' for Murren, Wengen, and so on. The permutations of this superb railway game never fail to fascinate.

The 'Orient' and 'Karlovy Vary' expresses were detached at Chalons but in those days the big reshuffle came at Chaumont, when from 11.10 to 11.30 pm the 'Tyrol,' 'Engadine' and 'Oberland' (and three times a week the 'Arlberg-Orient') expresses from Paris were dovetailed in with the Calais cars, the diner detached and the whole caravan sent on its way. A 15-minute stop was considered sufficient for Swiss formalities at Basle. Today, a longer stop is needed, but this includes the reshuffling process, whereby trains (mostly of ordinary carriages) from Paris, from

Calais and from Belgium are dealt in turn to other trains leaving for Bern and the Lötschberg route, for the Gotthard tunnel and Italy, and for eastern Switzerland and Austria. The carriages are loose-shunted into the various platforms complete with passengers on board; they glide down on their own, a blue-smocked shunter at the brake, after a kick from the shunting engine. All nations except the careful Swiss confine this kind of maneuver to freight cars; so it is worth waking up for, that much the more because such a rarity.

But all the indecent haste of 40 years ago was not much advantage to Davos passengers because, once the Austrian Tyrol and Arlberg cars were detached at Sargans (then to run through a whole sovereign state – little Leichtenstein – without stopping), the rest then had to be put aside for an hour or two so that Davos passengers could de-train at a reasonable hour (7.09 am) at Land-quart. Only on its final 20-mile run to Landquart and the end of standard gauge at Chur could the 'Engadine Express' heave a sigh of relief and say to itself, 'Alone at last, now I'm really a train.' Incidentally, arrival at St Anton by the 'Tyrol Express' branch of this train was then $2\frac{1}{2}$ hours earlier than it is now.

All this would have been only of academic interest to the Hollingsworth family, were it not that between the wars second-class passengers were admitted to the blue steel (but then occasionally still varnished teak) cars of the *Compagnie Internationale des Wagons-Lit et des Grands Express Européens*, whose glory has now almost departed. But having wept our tears, we can now dry them, for there are compensations. . . .

Until recent years, a journey to Switzerland via Harwich and the Hook of Holland was not specially convenient, but as the French route has deteriorated, the German one has improved. British Rail still keeps up a certain standard in the 'Hook Continental' evening boat train from London's Liverpool Street station, and the miniature liners which cross the North Sea are a pleasure to travel in. The cuisine, comfort and efficiency of the 'Rheingold Express' (at present first-class only – but there are rumors of a change), is unfaultable. The ride up the Rhine from Koblenz to Mainz is one of the great scenic journeys of the world and, if one finds a quiet moment to shift his bags from a Hook of Holland-Geneva coach to the Amsterdam-Chur one (which came on at Utrecht), there is no need to leave the train all the way to Landquart. Davos is reached almost exactly 24 hours after leaving Liverpool Street.

A crafty route which one can enjoy involves taking the Brussels car of the 'Night Ferry' train from Victoria and then taking a walk along the corridor before reaching Lille at 0626 hours, and so (in an ordinary train again without pretensions of any kind) put one's foot onto Swiss soil from England without ever touching anyone else's in between. If one has time one can alight at Mul-house, 21 miles from Basle, and visit the superb French Railways' Museum there. Davos can still

The 'Rheingold' express of the German Federal Railways at speed near Boppard in the Rhine Valley.

be reached the same night. During one incredible season in the 1960s, the 'Night Ferry' and this same connecting train actually carried a through Victoria-Basle car – the writer once travelled home in it and found it most satisfactory.

It is also possible even today to take one of the day sailings from Dover to Ostend and find at Ostend a sleeping car, belonging to *Wagons-Lits'* unglamorous successor *Trans-Europ-Nuit*, which will run through to Landquart via Brussels.

Perhaps the reader is wondering what the title of this piece has to do with its contents, because so far nothing has been said of either Crocodiles or Christies. Crocodiles began at Landquart. This was, and is, the name given to the brown and brassy older electric locomotives of the Rhaetian Railways, the meter-gauge independent network serving the southeast corner of Switzerland, better known perhaps as the *Rhätische Bahn* or RhB. More accurately they should be called 'baby

crocodiles' to distinguish them from similar standard-gauge machines belonging to big brother Swiss Federal. The name reflects the appearance: the windows of the cabs of these locomotives appear to examine viewers down a long and rather sinister nose. Nevertheless, they are extremely attractive.

'Christie' is short for Christiania Turn and it is the standard way of changing direction on skis. (Christiania, of course, is the old name for Oslo.) One might again ask what skiing has to do with rail travel and, in most of the world's ski resorts the answer is, not much; but Davos is different. The reason becomes apparent as one climbs from

1730ft altitude at Landquart to 5162ft at Davos. The Rhaetian is one of the boldest and most spectacular mountain railways ever to have been built, and its trains are doing 'Christies' all the way up (and down).

Seventy years ago 2–8–0 steam locomotives would have made it to Davos in 140 minutes from Landquart. Forty years ago a 'baby crocodile' would have needed 80. Since then newer (but duller) dark-green bogie locomotives have reduced this to 65, fairly reasonable for a 30-mile narrow-gauge ride, most of which is spent climbing at a hideous 1 in 22½. The journey can in fact still be made by all three generations of motive power – the crocodiles on stopping trains, and the 2–8–0s on occasional 'enthusiast' specials.

As it leaves Landquart, our train turns east into a valley called the Pratigau; the peaks on its north side are on the Austrian border, but those on the south form the legendary Parsenn ski area. The stations, Jenaz, Fideris, Küblis, Serneus, Saas, Klosters, Cavadürli, Laret, and Wolfgang are the end-points of famous Parsenn ski runs and are familiar to generations of holiday skiers from around the world. Cavadürli is a special favorite because one can ski out of the woods onto the station, and then put the signals at danger (there

is a button to press on the platform) to stop the next train.

To ski one of the runs one takes the Davos Parsennbahn up from Davos to the 9341ft summit of the Weissfluh mountain. Of all the rope (or funicular) railways in the world, the Parsenn Railway has an unbeaten combination of capacity and length. It is also one of the very few to run trains – in this case two cars coupled together – rather than single vehicles, carrying up to 170 passengers. It was built in the inauspicious year of 1931 to open up one of the world's greatest ski areas. Before this time the climb to over 9000ft altitude involved several hours walking with seal-skin strips strapped to one's skis. Nowadays during the season in spite of the continuous running, all seats strapped up out of use to allow more standing room and a ruthless people-packing system, a journey is the ultimate degree in crowded train travel. Added hazards of the DPB include platforms in the form of steep flights of steps (often ice-covered) and there is a hectic 'all-change' scramble between the first and second sections at the half-way point; moreover, participants are encumbered with skis and poles instead of briefcases, newspapers, knapsacks and suitcases.

As one train goes up another comes down on each section; the passing loop in the center is formed from fascinating switchless turnouts. Their working is a puzzle until one realizes that the cars have a double-flanged wheel on one side and a broad roller on the other. One set has the flanged wheels on the left side and the other has them on the right.

Climbing by Parsennbahn might be a rather masochistic form of pleasure, but skiing down on a fine day is an unbeatable thrill, made even better by the prospect of yet another ride on the RhB afterwards. A few years ago wise skiers ended their skiing day at Küblis, from where most conveniently the one-and-only *Schnellzug-mit-Speisewagen* (Restaurant Car Express) on the Davos line could be caught. Never did the giant block bells (wound up like grandfather clocks) on the platform ring out a blither peal than when announcing this one! RhB diners can be recognized by their color – the crimson lake of the prewar Mitropa company which originally supplied them; today they work the St Moritz line.

A Crococile-type narrow-gauge electric locomotive of the Rhaetian Railway, as used on ski trains to Davos.

Left:
Steam rotary snowplow of the Swiss Rhaetian Railway is propelled by a 2–8–0 steam locomotive.

Below:
A train of the Swiss Rhaetian Railway makes a conditional stop at Cavadürli to pick up skiers, who had set the signals at stop.

Bottom:
A Bernina Bahn train waits at Bernina Hospice station – note the trench cut by a rotary plow as well as the skier arriving for return transport to St Moritz by train.

Above:
The celebratory steam
special of the Swiss
Rhaetian Railway is hauled
by 2–8–0 steam locomotive
No 108, run in connection
with the centenary of the
town of Davos in February
1965.

'You never had it so good' applies to the RhB today and one should drag oneself away from the ski slopes and make a side-trip to fabled St Moritz, seeing en route engineering that is one of the railway wonders of the world. The little link train from Davos to Filisur is the kind of working on which the 'Crocodiles' are now found; at Filisur the St Moritz main line is joined. Soon a fast-running express enters the first of four spiral tunnels. Then, with a quite bewildering series of coils and loops, the railway manages to keep above the steeply rising floor of the valley – until finally it has to give up and drives through into the Engadine (and, incidentally, from country which drains into the North Sea to that which drains into the Danube and so the Black Sea) via the $4\frac{1}{2}$-mile Albula tunnel.

Samedan (change for Pontresina and Schuls-Tarasp) is the first stop in the wide, sunny Engadine valley and St Moritz is reached 20 minutes later. Note the bridge over the famous Cresta Run just after leaving Celerina. RhB trains also run from St Moritz via the 7400ft Bernina Pass down into Italy; this line, the old Bernina Railway, is more of a streetcar line; it has low-voltage DC traction instead of high-voltage AC, much sharper curves than the main RhB lines, and gradients which reach an extreme of 1 in 14. The 4000ft descent from Alp Grüm to Poschiavo is one of the world's most spectacular rail rides, although, with such curves and grades, obstacles that would otherwise mean heavy engineering works were

easily circumvented. The RhB then makes itself international by running those last few miles to Tirano in Italy; from there connections are available to Milan and the world beyond.

Another tentacle put out by the system is the famous 'Glacier Express' (complete with RhB dining car) from St Moritz right across Switzerland, 167 miles to Brig and Zermatt, in conjunction with the meter-gauge Furka-Oberalp and Brig-Visp-Zermatt railways; connection is made with the former at Disentis in the Lower Rhine valley. The 'Glacier Express' runs only in summer; at present it is physically prevented from doing so in winter, since the line over the Furka Pass is closed then. However, the $9\frac{3}{4}$-mile Furka 'base-tunnel' now being bored will allow this important cross-country link to operate all the year round by about 1982.

Always when the time came for the Hollings-worths to return to the real world – it seemed that railway and skiing holidays at Davos were as near Heaven as one would ever be likely to get – it was with great sadness. In the old days there was just one brief interlude to compensate; this was the 1 in 30 climb from Folkestone Harbour to Fole-stone Town with three (sometimes four) 0–6–0 tank locomotives front and rear. A tremendous whistling – so that all the drivers opened up together – heralded a display of everything that made steam operation of railways such an heroic affair. Even Kent, the 'Garden of England,' provided its own railway mountaineering.

Above:
Furka-Oberalp Bahn steam-hauled ski train ascends the rack incline from Andermatt to Natschen.

Left:
Two views of the Folkestone to London. Continental Express leaving Folkestone Harbour for Folkestone Town – note three ex-Great Western pannier tank locomotives, two in front, one at rear, provided for the 1 in 30 climb.

Route 8
The Immortal 'Orient Express'

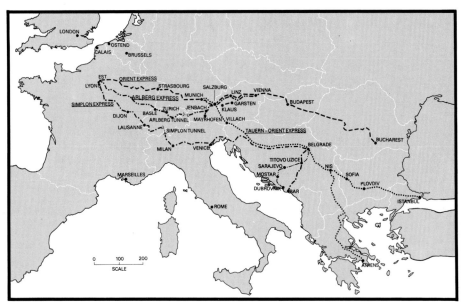

Ever since Marlene Dietrich trod its corridors on the silver screen, the 'Orient Express' has been linked with the kind of spy thriller in which the hero is given up for dead – gassed, gagged, bound and left to his fate in one of its sleeping cars – and yet returns fit and well to annihilate the 'baddies' in the last chapter. The train itself is a little like that. Wars have put it out of action for years at a time, and even in peacetime its recent funeral was celebrated with great ceremony, back in 1976 – yet if you went now to the Gare de L'Est in Paris late in the evening on a Monday, Wednesday, Friday or Saturday, you could step into a sleeping car of the 'Orient Express' for Bucharest just as you could (only once a week then) back in 1883 when the train ran for the first time. Then as now there neither were nor are through cars for Istanbul, although nowadays the Russian Moscow-Istanbul car can be taken on from Bucharest once a week.

Breakfast and lunch can be enjoyed in a dining car which runs from Stuttgart to Vienna and dinner in another from Hegyeshalom (on the Austria-Hungary frontier) to Budapest. No doubt the sleeping-car conductor can do something

about breakfast next morning – arrival in Bucharest is in time for a late lunch. The overall time of 34 hours 15 minutes (average 44mph) today compares quite favorably with the 52 hours of the 1883 schedule; all in all it is an easy and comfortable journey in a very respectable train, provided one's visa is in order.

One should wake up the first morning in one of the nicest parts of Germany – Bavaria – and at mid-day enter Austria at Salzburg; in the afternoon comes all the ordeal of crossing the Iron Curtain, but the pleasure of seeing the occasional choice steam locomotive is compensation. Hungarian steam includes modern 4–8–0s, medium age 2–6–2s, 2–6–2Ts and 2–4–2Ts, and really ancient (but still efficient) 0–6–0s and 0–6–0Ts, all kept in good order. Austria also has some steam as do Rumania and Bulgaria but none is likely to be seen on the 'Orient Express' route.

As is well known, the original train had tentacles which went all over Europe. The author introduced the reader to the Calais branch earlier, incongruously attached to a winter-sports express. Ostend, Brussels, Frankfurt, Basle, Zürich, Milan, Venice, Belgrade, Athens and, of course, Istanbul

were additional places served by cars running on the 'Arlberg-Orient,' 'Simplon-Orient' and 'Ostend-Vienna-Orient' expresses. Their aristocratic origin has not prevented these children from making their way in a plebian world, dropping their parents' name in doing so. So the 'Simplon' and 'Arlberg' expresses still work the first part of their courses out of Paris, but, like the 'Orient' itself, admit 'couchette' cars as well as first- and second-class ordinary coaches. Athens and Istanbul are now only served by the child of the 'Orient''s old age, the 'Tauern Orient,' which carries cars from Munich to Istanbul and Athens (a sleeping car runs to the latter twice weekly).

Of course, should one have wanted to go to the real Orient, the Far East, one would not have taken the 'Orient Express' or any of its children but the once-weekly all-sleeper 'Bombay Express' from Calais to Marseilles, run exclusively to connect with steamers of the Peninsula and Oriental Steam Navigation Company – the fabled P & O. In 1938 departure from Calais immediately followed that of the trains carrying the 'Orient' (or 'Arlberg-Orient') and 'Simplon-Orient' cars respectively. Marseilles was reached

Extreme left:
The 'Arlberg Express' on the Austrian Federal Railways Arlberg Main Line near Flirsch-am-Arlberg is hauled by electric locomotive No 1110.18.

Below:
Yugoslavian narrow-gauge – a freight train from Dubrovnik to Sarajevo negotiates the rack section between Bradina and Konic.

Bottom:
Zillertal Railway, Austria – locomotive No 2 *Zillertal* leaves Zell-am-Ziller with the 1010 train from Jenbach to Mayrhofen.

the following morning; no doubt those who could afford the overland journey also got the original POSH (Port Out, Starboard Home) shady cabins on the steamer.

The 'Simplon Express,' which leaves Paris in the early evening for Belgrade, is now a poor thing; there is no diner, only a buffet car, in France; there are no refreshments at all in Italy; and the Yugoslavian buffet car is not available until late afternoon. Both the Italians and the Yugoslavs have magnificent railway systems (to which it is admitted this book pays insufficient heed), but the 'Simplon Express' is not the way to find out about them. Both Italy and Yugoslavia also have the odd pocket of active steam.

The Yugoslavs have a deep appreciation of trains. Up until 20 years ago one could set out on a fantastic 28-hour 470-mile journey on the 2ft 6in gauge from Belgrade via Titovo Uzice, Visegrad, Sarajevo and Mostar to Dubrovnik. Between Titovo Uzice and Visegrad there were convolutions that rival those on the Albula line met earlier (Route 7), while beyond Mostar there were long sections of rack-and-pinion working.

Added spice was given to an already-interesting journey by the likelihood of trouble from the railway authorities, the uniformed police or the plainclothes men. The game of photographing Yugoslavian Railways is made more interesting by the fact that, if official permission to take pictures is obtained from one authority, the others redouble their efforts at harassment. Now, however, the narrow-gauge with its iron-clad security has gone. What did the Yugoslavs do? They offer instead a brand-new super-modern 320-mile Belgrade to Bar railway, driven through the mountains. Security on the new line is somewhat lax because various foreign government experts (British, German and Soviet amongst them) were consulted on the formidable engi-

neering problems; the 70 miles of tunnelling serve to rest the senses between startling vistas, including (among the nine miles of bridging) that from the highest railway bridge in the world, the Mala Rijeka viaduct, 613ft above its valley. It is a nine-hour trip which six trains make daily. Connections to Istanbul from Belgrade are now made (in this case after spending the night there) by the very basic 'Marmara Express' of which, perhaps, the less said the better.

The 'Arlberg Express' is rather a better train and always a favorite of the writer ever since, once long ago, he arrived an hour or so early to catch it coming west and caught the previous day's train instead. The late Bryan Morgan, in his most evocative book on train travel, *The End of the Line*, refers to that 'lightning of the heart which always accompanies crossing the border into Austria.' We left the 'Arlberg' in the last section doing just that thing; its occupants would know it was Austria because customs and immigration control people would be just grinning faces in the window with a thumbs-up sign. Once in the author's experience did a customs official enter the compartment here but only (with great apologies) to retrieve a bottle of Swiss 'fire-water' that had been left for him under the seat.

The ascent to the Arlberg tunnel is steep but not spectacular and soon enough the train is inside the 6.4-mile bore. Immediately on exit comes St Anton, a village where (until he fell out with Hitler) the great Hannes Schneider laid the foundations of modern skiing and its teaching. Around 10.30 pm each night he used to take a posse of ski-teachers round the night spots of St Anton; if any of his pupils were still there, it was assumed they did not wish to continue learning skiing the Arlberg way!

Although nowadays its discipline is not so fierce, the Arlberg Ski-School is still marvellous, but a

Right:
A local push-and-pull steam train enters Budapest West station in June 1975.

Extreme right:
On the 'Orient Express' a French courier in a sleeping car of the *Compagnie Internationale des Wagons Lits* exchanges diplomatic bags in Munich station.

beginner on skis might try a more modest place – one such is Mayrhofen. Mayrhofen has its own rather special little railway, the Zillertalbahn (ZB), to connect it with Jenbach on the Arlberg main line. ZB has run utilitarian diesel railcars for many years. In the old days little 0–6–2Ts plied up and down the beautiful snowy valley hauling typical end-gallery four-wheelers, warm and snug with their steam heat – there was even a mail van complete with post-horn insignia and letter box. To complement this mail van was Mayrhofen station itself which was opened by Emperor Franz Joseph in 1895.

Nowadays the steam fleet is used mainly to provide steam trains twice daily in summer for pleasure. However, something rather special is included – the opportunity of driving a steam train oneself. There is a need to book in advance (see appendix). This facility – shared only by one other railway in the whole world, also an Austrian 2ft 6in gauge (the Murtalbahn near Klagenfurt) – is advertised as operating from June to September. Outside this period it would be worth trying to talk the authorities into it – the charming Aus-

trians enjoy nothing better than making others happy.

Other enchanting 2ft 6in gauge railways abounded in Austria, but most are now dieselized, electrified or closed. Current exceptions are the Steyrtalbahn from Klaus to Garsten (descend from the 'Arlberg' or the 'Orient Express' at Linz and take the Selzthal train), and two branches at Gmund on the Czechoslovakian border, in the far northeast. Thus one arrives at Vienna in the evening, the best time for that wonderful city.

Although the 'Orient Express' no longer maintains its old hauteur and grandeur one can still make de-luxe journeys on a revived 'Orient Express.' Herr Albert Glatt, a Swiss who has acquired a fleet of the famous vehicles, occasionally runs them from Zürich or Lausanne (occasionally Frankfurt) via the Simplon or Arlberg routes to Istanbul or Athens. Participants go in one direction by air, the other by train, thus allowing two groups to be accommodated for each return trip of the train. Where possible, steam or vintage electric motive power is provided.

These 'Glattzug' expresses actually go one

The coaches of the 'Orient Express' are cleaned at Istanbul Sirekli Station.

better than the 'Orient Express' ever did (except the one in the film of Agatha Christie's detective story), because they have not only sleeping and dining cars but Pullman cars also; furthermore there is a gala dinner where one is expected to dress *en grande tenue*. In 1979 only one trip was run, outward to Istanbul via the 'Simplon-Orient' route (starting from Zürich). Return was via Bulgaria, Rumania, Czechoslovakia and Austria mostly by steam. This has rather a different appeal and one wonders whether our friend (to whom all lovers of *Madame La Compagnie* in any case should be eternally grateful) will manage to get steam fans to dress for dinner! Bookings to Intraflug A.G., Thomas Cook or a Swiss National Tourist Office.

In 1981 a second new 'Orient Express' will also combine the luxury and glamor of the original train in the heyday of the Twenties and Thirties with some additional modern conveniences of the 1980s. The 18-coach luxury train, with accommodation for 150 passengers, will travel regularly between London and Venice via Dunkirk, Paris, Lausanne, the Simplon tunnel in Switzer-land and Milan. The schedule of the trip is designed to make the most of daylight, so that the traveller can enjoy panoramic views of the impressive White Cliffs of Dover, the countryside of France and Italy, and the Swiss Alps.

To make up the train, vintage Pullman cars and *Wagons-Lits* are being brought out of retirement from all over Europe, including several from railway museums, and modified to modern operating standards. All are being furnished in the authentic 1920s style of the original train – with the staff wearing uniforms to match. *Haut cuisine* will be included in the fare – which roughly matches that of first-class air travel.

Up-to-date features will include refrigeration and air-conditioning, shower accommodation and telephones. The 'Express' will run via the Dover–Dunkirk train ferry with some of the Pullman cars running direct between London and Venice. The new train is the brainchild of a London company, Sea Containers Limited, and the famous Hotel Cipriani of Venice. It will operate in conjunction with the various national railways involved.

A candle-light dinner on the 'Orient Express' luxury 'for pleasure' revival, which occurs once or twice a year.

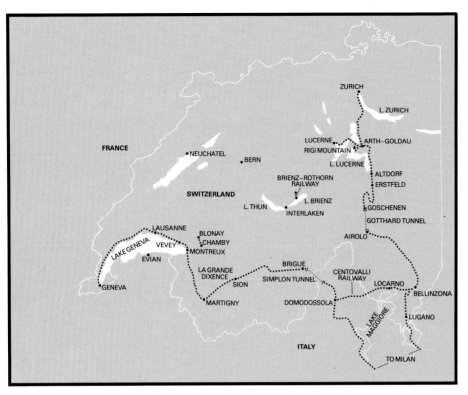

Route 9
Swiss Rails

There is no doubt that Switzerland possesses the best-integrated public transport in the world. Her railways form its basis and the services of trains, lake steamers, streetcars and buses are all carefully planned to inter-connect so as to make travel as convenient and trouble-free as possible. This is one reason why Swiss Federal Railways have never suffered anything like the sharp humiliation of a 'Beeching Axe' as has occurred in Britain, or the great 'co-ordination' of 1938 in France.

Moreover, for a country with four official languages and eleven political parties, the achievement of such transport integration is no mean feat.

Students of history will know that for centuries the Swiss were a belligerent nation. When they were not fighting each other they served as mercenaries in other countries' wars, and from time to time they were forced to repel invaders. However, just over 130 years ago in 1848, when the rest of Europe was aflame with revolution, the Swiss character underwent a significant change. Its citizens decided that aggression was a waste of time. Be it for religious, political or territorial aims, it dawned on the Swiss that nobody ever really won a war and the cost in terms of human suffering and destruction of property was pure insanity.

Accordingly, all the semi-autonomous Cantons were welded into one republic as the 'Helvetian Confederation.' From then the Swiss set about the task of making their small country as pleasant as possible for themselves and for their visitors, whose peaceful invasion was so ably led by Great Britain's own Thomas Cook.

Two factors vitally affected the construction and operation of Switzerland's railways: firstly, nature and, secondly, the geographical position of the country. The Confederation is in the center of Western Europe and shares borders with four other lands.

Nature has proved to be a two-edged sword. On the one hand she has given visitors views of dramatic beauty which are unsurpassed in Europe, but *per contra* nature has posed problems which most railway engineers would have declared impossible to surmount. Very early in their experience Swiss railway constructors learned to delete the word 'impossible' from their vocabulary.

Later, as the Railway Age progressed and the steel ribbons began to spread over Europe, the Swiss were forced to realize that they had to operate what the Americans call a series of 'bridge routes.' Their railways were not merely a domestic matter, as for example, they were in Britain. On the contrary, the Swiss found themselves the 'Clapham Junction' of Western Europe. Almost every European nation needed to use Swiss metals in order to trade with or visit other nations; for example, if one haunts the great station of Basle for 24 hours, one can spot expresses leaving for no less than 17 separate countries in Europe.

Switzerland entered the railway scene rather late. Her first line was a local one of a mere 15 miles between Zürich and Baden, which opened in 1847, 17 years later than the world's first passenger-carrying steam railway between Liverpool and Manchester.

Despite this late start, the savage terrain and the blistering difficulties of winter snows, Swiss railway construction went ahead doggedly yet imaginatively and rapidly. By the turn of the century almost 2500 route-miles of track were open to traffic, that is to say about 75 percent of the present system.

A few more facts about Swiss Federal Railways are important. An ordinary return ticket only costs one-and-a-half times the return fare instead of double as in most countries. Many money-saving tickets are available to visitors and details can be obtained from Swiss National Tourist Offices in 25 countries around the world. These facilities include combinations of flying, local car rentals and passes for unlimited travel in a particular zone or over the entire Swiss railway system.

The interiors of all Swiss trains are kept clean including the toilets. When there is no restaurant car with full meal service, all medium and long-distance trains have a 'mini buffet' or ambulant trolley to provide snacks and hot and cold drinks. Swiss station restaurants offer a wide selection of meals at reasonable prices and even people who seldom travel by train frequently patronize them.

Most Swiss railways were nationalized by 1909, although to this day a number of private railway companies, not by any means all branch-like outfits co-exist on a friendly yet competitive basis. Perhaps the most unusual characteristic of Swiss railways is that they do not have rail strikes; the public can completely rely on railways. Why is this so? Because as long ago as 1936 Swiss management and workers got together and decided that strikes – like wars – never benefited anyone on either side. Accordingly, the contract between the top brass and the humblest shunter is a legal document, lasting for three years; if either party breaks it he is sent to prison. Each agreement cannot be altered in law without three recourses to an independent arbitration, the last of which must be held publicly in the Swiss Parliament.

One of Switzerland's most interesting railways is the Gotthard Line. Strictly speaking this line begins in Lucerne and ends at Chiasso on the border with Italy. It is Switzerland's most dramatic route and was the most difficult, most dangerous and most expensive to build. The cost of piercing the implacable Alps was heavy in men and materials and no less than 177 workers (many of them Italian) suffered fatal accidents during construction. Their sculpted memorial stands in Airolo station.

The *chef d'oeuvre* of the mountain section is, of course, the main Gotthard tunnel itself – the world's second longest – at just over nine miles through solid rock. But, in addition, there are 80 other tunnels and 79 bridges and viaducts. The Gotthard Line was first mooted as early as 1860 but due to the difficulty of the terrain and the vast expense involved, progress was slow. Eventually, a Swiss-German-Italian consortium was formed and work on the great tunnel began in 1872. Boring began at both ends simultaneously with an average daily workforce of 2500 men.

Conditions were appalling; tunnelling equipment was primitive, safety precautions were few and rockfalls and underground springs all contributed to the casualties. Finally, at the end of February 1880 after eight years of gruelling toil, the breakthrough was made and the two bores met mid-mountain. They were out of alignment by only 15 inches horizontally and a mere 2 inches vertically – an astonishing tribute to the skill of engineers and workmen of a century ago.

Two years later the whole line was completed and opened to traffic. For 40 years, until electrification in 1922, all trains were steam-hauled. Conditions in the tunnels were not pleasant for the passengers but for the locomotive crews they were just about the nearest thing to Hell itself. Accordingly, for working between Erstfeld and Bellinzona (the most difficult section) a stud of specially maintained locomotives and specially trained crews was kept on hand, for the company dared not risk the disaster of a train stalling in any of the tunnels. Nowadays, with electric locomotives of up to 12,000hp such precautions are unnecessary.

The journey begins tranquilly enough. Leaving the terminus of Lucerne the line skirts the north shore of the lake, giving magnificent views across it. (No visitor to Lucerne should fail to visit the Swiss Transport Museum which houses a fine collection of railway relics, vintage motor cars

Bern-Lötschberg-Simplon Railway's 'Blue Arrow' electric train runs alongside Lake Thun between Speiz and Interlaken.

and aircraft.)

Next, the line passes the foot of the Rigi Mountain up whose steep slopes the famous Swiss engineer, Niklaus Riggenbach, built Europe's first rack-railway in 1871. Veering away from the strangely shaped lake for a while, the line regains the east shore as far as the town of Altdorf, where the over-life-size figures of William Tell and his plucky son overlook the market-place. Soon the climbing begins in earnest with three spiral tunnels near Wassen leading to the final climb high up the side of a mountain and as the lowlands disappear the train halts at Göschenen, the last station before the Gotthard tunnel.

Here one finds a surprisingly large station buffet because, in the days of steam traction, a lengthy stop was made for passengers to fortify themselves before undergoing the rigors of the nine-mile smoke-filled tunnel. Nowadays most through trains roar through non-stop. The run through the tunnel itself is not very interesting although the sudden exit into breath-taking scenery is more than ample compensation.

Emerging into daylight – and it has taken only some 15 minutes to pierce the mountain – one arrives at Airolo. This is in Ticino, Switzerland's Italian-speaking Canton, and the houses and countryside now take on a more Italian appearance as one moves south. There are still four more tunnels, all spiral ones, to negotiate before reaching the lovely lakeside city of Lugano. This is a good place to end the Gotthard excursion, except for those who want to continue into Italy.

Few words have been wasted in describing the awe-inspiring scenery on show since leaving Lucerne simply because mere words are totally inadequate. The Gotthard Railway offers a journey that everyone ought to experience once in a lifetime. The alpine spectacles and the feats of engineering are all classics. In fact, the Gotthard is quite simply the finest mountain rail line in the world. Any person disposed to doubt this need do no more, for example, than take a seat in a Gotthard diner and time his meal to coincide with the mountain crossing. The train, weighing some 500 tons perhaps, will surge effortlessly

Swiss Federal Railways sponsor an old-time train formed of original and replica stock of the Spanish-Bun-Railway, the first line lying wholly in Switzerland to be completed. It ran from Zürich to Baden.

up the three percent grades, banking heavily into the curves at a steady 50mph. The wine waiter will stand to fill your glass, pouring fast and firmly, and never spill a drop as you roar out of one corkscrew tunnel and into the next.

Swiss Federal Railway's Lausanne to Bern express in winter.

One of the best stations from which to explore Switzerland by rail is Brig, since one can go in four different directions, each of which reveals a different aspect of this small republic. The best-known journey from Brig is the Simplon Line, including as it does the world's longest railway tunnel with a length of almost 12½ miles.

The Simplon Pass is no newcomer to history for the original route over the mountains was hewn out by the Romans in 196 BC. Centuries later it was much improved by Napoleon Bonaparte who was always keen to build roads in other countries, including Switzerland, for strategic purposes. (One of the Emperor's lesser-known sayings is: 'So far as I am concerned the word "neutrality" has no meaning.')

A railway under the Simplon Pass, linking western Switzerland with Italy, was promoted some years later than the Gotthard. One prime question was whether to go for a relatively short tunnel at high altitude with steep gradients to reach it, or alternatively, to construct a longer low-level tunnel with more gentle approaches. Finally, after many Swiss-Italian consultations the latter course was adopted.

Work began on a single-track bore in 1898, again from both ends at once. Due to the unprecedented length a second small tunnel, only 8ft in diameter, was built alongside for ventilation purposes and connected cross-wise at intervals of 200 yards. Later in 1912, due to a further increase in traffic this parallel shaft was enlarged to full size so that the track could be doubled.

The Simplon tunnel crosses the frontier into Italy almost halfway along its length. Emerging from the southern portal the traveller soon finds

himself in Domodossola. Here he can change trains and explore the Centovalli Line which runs half in Switzerland and half in Italy through wildly beautiful country to lovely Locarno on Lake Maggiore. Alternatively he can sit tight past Domodossola until he reaches the town of Stresa on the southwest shore of Lake Maggiore. From here he may take a motorboat to visit the fabulous Isola Bella with its fairylike palace and formal gardens, the latter patrolled by white peacocks.

True, the Simplon Line is not as dramatic as the Gotthard, but nevertheless it comprises four other tunnels and 19 bridges and snow-galleries.

There is a variety of ways to make the Simplon trip. One can simply take an ordinary train. On the other hand it can be done *de luxe* in one of the famous named trains such as the 'Simplon Express' or, to enjoy the ultimate luxury of modern rail travel, by two Trans-European Expresses, the 'Lemano' (Geneva-Milan) or the 'Cisalpin' (Paris-Milan).

Electrification came somewhat late by Swiss standards to this route; it was not completed over the whole stretch until 1930, although the Simplon tunnel itself was electrified from the outset.

Should one catch one of the trains from Brig heading westward, one will find oneself following the Rhône valley, surrounded by peaks on either side, until one reaches Martigny. Here the train and the river head northwest until they reach the splendidly set Lake Geneva. Almost at once between the tracks and the water looms up the grim medieval Chateau de Chillon, immortalized by the poet Byron and a reminder of Switzerland's less democratic days when her political prisoners were imprisoned forever. On one of his otherwise happy visits to Switzerland, Charles Dickens noted with horror the chute down which prisoners' bodies were pushed into the lake but even then the chute was a museum piece.

A couple of miles further on, in the pretty little town of Territet, in the main street, there is a sculptured monument to the Empress Elizabeth of Austria-Hungary, wife of the venerable Emperor Franz Josef who ruled from 1848 until 1916. On a sunny September day in 1898 when Elizabeth was on holiday incognito in Geneva she decided to take one of her many solitary, escapist excursions, in this case, the lake steamer from Territet to visit her friends the Rothchilds at nearby Pregny. As she walked from the Hôtel Beau Rivage, accompanied only by a lady-in-waiting, towards the boat, she was fatally stabbed by an Italian anarchist. This tragic event was most embarrassing for the Swiss Government which ought to have taken tighter security precautions and that is, perhaps, why there is no monument to Elizabeth in Geneva – just this modest one in Territet.

After Territet comes Montreux, a popular holiday center and formerly the most 'British' area in the country. (This was because, before World War II when the pound sterling was

Swiss Federal Railway's 1–C–C–1 Crocodile-type electric locomotive heads a special train provided to view the Muttenz marshalling yards at Basle.

top right :

Railway lineside 'furniture' is becoming more and more popular as exterior decor. At Trubschachen, near Bern, the owner of the Hotel Bahnhof displays (from left to right) : a buffer-stop, a station bell, an upper quadrant semaphore signal, a point indicator and a level crossing barrier.

bottom Right :

Brienz–Rothorn Railway's steam-propelled trains on the ascent.

Europe's strongest currency, many not-so-well-off Britons retired here to escape the rigors of their native country's winters and her taxation.) Montreux is also an excellent place from which to explore other parts of Switzerland by rail : there are many delightful local mountain trips and the Bernese Oberland is within easy reach.

The next large town is Vevey which (surprisingly) possesses a fine Russian Orthodox church, built by refugees who were fortunate enough to escape into Switzerland from the revolution of 1917. For the traveller who is interested in vintage railways, both steam and electric, a short deviation northwards will take him to Switzerland's preserved tourist line, the Blonay-Chamby Railway. Here is a variety of motive power and rolling stock, not only of Swiss origin but from other countries as well. There is also a fine museum, not to mention spectacular views of the lake. The line operates every weekend from Easter to October.

Continuing westwards the line stays near the lake and as the track is so level and straight one can hustle along on one of Switzerland's few railway 'galloping grounds.' Lausanne, a very feminine city and the seat of the Supreme Court of Justice, is soon reached. On a clear day the well-known French resort of Evian can be seen across the water while immediately on the right are the extensive vineyards of the Canton of Vaud. Finally, and less than three hours' run from Brig, is Geneva itself, the least *Swiss* city in the Confederation because it is so international. Now the seat of so many international organizations and the scene of so many international conferences, Geneva has lost much of its 'Swissness' but retains much of its charm especially in the Old Town.

Closer to Brig one can experience an utterly different kind of journey. Just as the County of Kent is considered the 'Garden of England,' the Canton of Valais is considered the 'Garden of Switzerland.' Geographically speaking this area is like a fishbone. The central part is the east-west route from Brig to Martigny, running down the wide valley of the River Rhône, while the cross-vertebrae are the numerous little valleys that penetrate north and south into the mountains on either side of the river.

On the south slopes grow some of Switzerland's most famous wines and the valley floor produces fruit and vegetables in profusion. This is one of the bilingual Cantons; in the eastern half the official language is German and in the western part French. In practise almost everyone speaks both.

On this run one does not encounter a single tunnel or bridge worth mentioning; it is a level line through lush colorful country which in summer it is very hot.

Anyone with time to spare should not fail to stop off and explore some of the minor valleys. Most fascinating of all is the Val d'Hérémence. As there is no railway one takes the yellow Post Bus from Sion and it is a hair-raising ride. There are innumerable hairpin bends, some grisly,

dripping tunnels (all very short) and all the time one gets a loftier birds-eye view of the main valley below.

About half-way, one passes the 'Swiss Pyramids,' a number of quite extraordinary conical rock formations, some of which have a huge stone precariously balanced on top. These are the results of harsh winter weather on different consistencies of rock over thousands of years. But the greatest visual shock is still to come – it is Switzerland's vast dam for hydroelectric power, the Barrage de la Grande Dixence.

As the bus swings round the last of the bends and emerges from the last tunnel, passengers can see – almost on top of them, it seems – the gigantic concrete wall built between two mountains to hold back millions of tons of water, destined to feed the turbines which supply the ever-increasing demand for electric power.

Characteristically, one also finds a technical museum, a hotel with restaurant and a small chapel, the latter dedicated to the engineers and workers who built this astonishing monument to electricity.

No visit to the alpine country of Switzerland could be complete without experiencing at least one of her rack railways. (The Swiss did not invent these – the first was, and curiously enough still is, in the United States – but they have certainly made them their own.)

As Swiss tourism burgeoned in the late 1860s it became all too obvious that mules and *chaises-à-porteurs* were hopelessly inadequate to carry the thousands of people who now wanted to reach the tops of Swiss mountains.

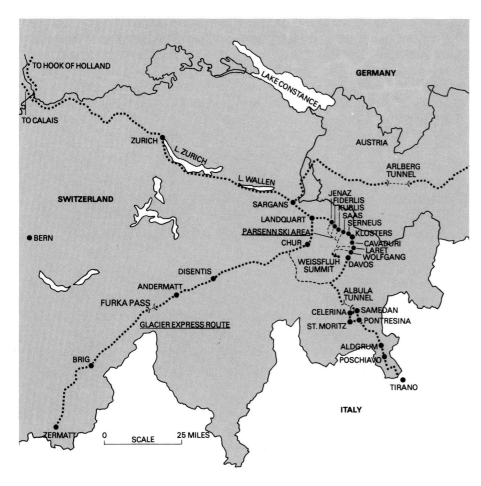

Europe's first mountain railway up the mighty Rigi (5896ft to the top) was built by the distinguished Swiss engineer, Niklaus Riggenbach. Faced with vertiginous gradients on which no ordinary train could hope to get a grip, Riggenbach conceived the idea of the locomotive with a cog-wheel engaging in a steel 'ladder' between the lines. Curiously enough, sometimes great inventions coincide, since Riggenbach's ladder-rack is very like that used by the American engineer Marsh on his pioneer line up Mount Washington.

Having reached the top of the Rigi mountain by Riggenbach's line, as a bonus, one can descend by another rack railway to Arth-Goldau on the opposite side of the mountain.

Lastly, the other rack line which is a 'must' (though there are dozens more) is the Brienz-Rothorn Railway. This climbs from the Lake of Brienz to a height of 7707 feet and it is Switzerland's last public railway to be even partly operated by steam locomotives, although in 1977 two diesel locomotives were experimentally introduced. It is hardly necessary to add that, as the trains ascend these dizzy heights one gets a more and more staggering view of the lakes and valleys below. Faced with these near-Heavenly sights and heights, it is perhaps comforting to know that these railways are annually inspected by government experts to ensure safety!

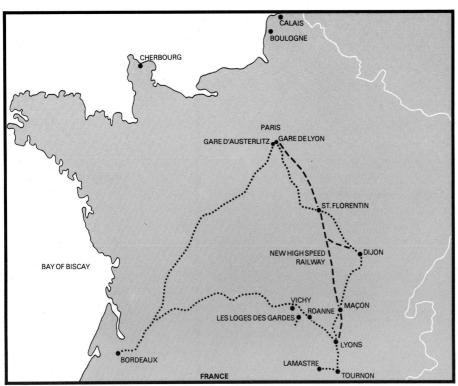

Route 10 French Connections

One should begin one's exploration of the French railways at the Gare de Lyon in Paris near lunch time. Awaiting custom is 'Le Mistral,' first-class only with supplementary charge, ready to make the run down the great main line of the old Paris-Lyon-Mediterranée Company (PLM). Apart from the extra-on-extra cost, the only unpleasant thing about it is its name. The Mistral is a justly hated wind which spoils the amenities of the Côte d'Azur.

'Le Mistral''s predecessor, the winter-only 'Côte d'Azur Pullman' of the PLM line's fabulous steamy past, while also lacking nothing in comfort, took one hour 25 minutes longer to Lyon.

Although one might lament its passing, especially the glorious machinery which did the honors at the front end, the absence of smuts is a solid achievement in favor of the all-electric 'Mistral.'

If one can bear to lift his eyes from the *haute cuisine* lunch that is served as the afternoon wears on (arguably the best on any train anywhere) one might see new scars on the hills. These are not for the usual Autoroute but for the new Paris-Lyon high-speed railway. With trains running at up to 160mph, it is intended that the Paris-Lyon running time will be improved a further one hour and 47 minutes to a straight two hours. The first section expected to open will be from St Florentin to Lyon in 1981. It will be an exciting ride.

Soon names familiar from wine lists begin to flash past on station name boards and this writer for one touches his hat to them, not only out of respect for the great Burgundian vineyards but also in gratitude for something else. Imagine a wine-waiter at a distinguished restaurant presenting a *formidable carte des vins* to a diffident young man whose ignorance about wine was abysmal. How to select with even the semblance of confidence from these pages of names? The answer was simple; wine has to be carried to market – often in France by rail tank cars – and so many of the wine names are also railway names. So, it was easy to bring an informed judgment to choose on the basis of wheel-arrangement or rail gauge, rather than flavor or bouquet. The system worked – interesting wine and interesting railways have an affinity!

Forty years ago, when local trains in Britain and Germany had still another 20 years in which to remain steam, French lines were already the province of the famous autorails or railcars. Our

run down the unfashionable right bank of the Rhône to Tournon is an opportunity to try just such a conveyance. The 'Mistral,' like the 'Rheingold,' takes the railway on the left bank. But Tournon on the right bank is the place where the best steam 'fix' in the whole of France can be found: the famous Réseau de Vivarais.

Until their closure in 1959, the Vivarais lines had served the superb country west of the Rhône valley with 120 or so miles of wonderful narrow-gauge mountain railway. Taking their example from what had been done across the Channel, a group of railway enthusiasts were able, in 1965, to take over (after a good deal of bureaucratic haggling) a 20-mile section based at Tournon. The best day for a visit is a summer Sunday, when some of the original Mallet tank locomotives and other steam power are in action. Series of trains make their way to Lamastre at the other end of the preserved section, up some splendid rocky defiles, for that great French institution, Sunday lunch in a good restaurant. Steam and good living are a great combination and the time-table is arranged so that no one's digestion is disturbed. (One always hopes the engine crew will not be too somnolent approaching Tournon on

Above:
A French National Railways' dining car of the 'Mistral' express.

Left:
The 'Mistral' express at speed.

the return journey, for the trains run through a tunnel against the current of traffic on a mixed gauge arrangement using one of the SNCF tracks.)

For the next day's entertainment, the recommendation is an autorail ride (change at Lyon) north and then west to the town of Roanne, reached at mid-day. Near here some brave souls have spiked down a bit of the old Wild West in one of the most picturesque parts of *La Belle France*. The line runs up in the mountains between Roanne and Vichy at a place called Les Loges des Gardes – in contrast to the Vivarais it is not a revival but a new creation. The locomotive and train is a half-size steam replica of the standard and legendary American diamond-stack wooden cab 4–4–0; as for the rolling stock, one instinctively looks for Indian arrows in the woodwork.

Roanne is worth visiting for another and particularly French reason: the little town – one of

only eleven in the whole of France – is distinguished by a restaurant which has earned the top accolade of three rosettes. *The Michelin Guide* says quite simply 'Here one will find the best cooking in France, worthy of a special journey.' The Hôtel des Frères Trigros is in La Place du Gare (indeed, the station actually appears on the menu) and it provides accommodation as well as food. But it is a question of booking dinner well ahead.

Next morning, to conclude this French tour, one might return to Paris making a considerable detour. One can ride one of the French turbo-trains across the wonderful Massif Central to Bordeaux and then return to Paris (Austerlitz) on the train which makes what is nowadays the longest non-stop run in the world (363 miles), averaging 94mph while doing it. This is 'L'Etendard.' The timetable for the day is: Roanne depart 0739; Bordeaux, arrive 1355; Bordeaux, depart 1750; Paris (Austerlitz) arrive 2140hrs.

Above:
La Loge des Gardes
Railway's half-size replica
'Wild West' American
4–4–0. Note appropriate
rolling stock, buildings and
scenery.

Right:
French National Railways
'Etendard' express about to
leave Paris Austerlitz
station.

Left:
French National Railways
in steam days – a magnificent
compound 4–8–2 locomotive
of class 241P at Nevers.

Below:
Reseau du Vivarais mallet
0–6–6–0T in pre-
preservation days, at
Dunières. This locomotive
now works tourist trains at
weekends between Tournon
on the Rhône and Lamastre.

Soviet Union

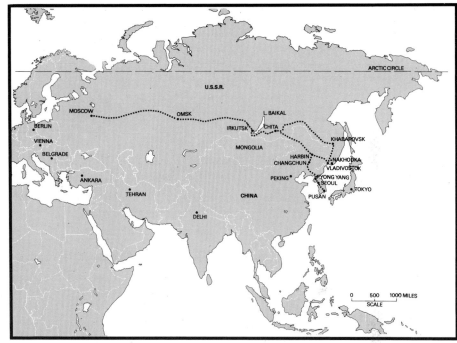

On most counts the 85,000-mile Soviet railway system is the largest in the world – unless, of course, the USA's many companies are grouped together as a single unit. In respect of freight traffic, the Soviet system does more haulage than the rest of the world put together. However, regarding the volume of passenger traffic, the system has several rivals – notably Japan and India. People in the USSR tend to be less highly regarded than freight when it comes to railroads. There certainly seems no question of enough spare capacity for people on the USSR's railways – either native or foreign – but security and custom do not allow anyone just to jump on a train. In fact, foreigners are very rarely offered any journey other than one far too famous one.

So, in following the procedure of describing a journey which illustrates the ambience of passenger travel in any country, a problem is encountered and it is this. In addition to having the largest railway system the USSR also runs a train which, by a factor of two, makes the longest journey in the world. Consequently very many travellers on what is popularly (but incorrectly) known as the 'Trans-Siberian Express,' have been unable to resist the temptation to write it into their memoirs. With this in mind, this writer feels unable to add anything to the many accounts he has read. But how to reconcile this with the fact that a piece on the Moscow-Vladivostok 'Russia Express' (that is the true name) is compulsory in any rail travel book? The solution is to set the journey not on the 'Russia' itself but through its literature.

But first a glance at the background. In the late years of the last century the rulers of Russia decided to strengthen their grip on their Siberian domains by building a railway to the Pacific Ocean. The first sod was cut at the Pacific port of Vladivostok in 1891 and through rail communication (of a sort, began in 1903. One must say 'of a sort' for three reasons. First, it was difficult enough to find the money for a railway which was longer than any which has ever been built, without adding to the burden by constructing it other than in the lightest possible way. Second, there was a gap, closed by a train ferry, across Lake Baikal and, third, the line ran direct from Harbin to Vladivostok across Chinese Manchuria.

The railway around the southern shore of Lake Baikal was completed in 1905 and the present less-direct route wholly on Soviet soil was completed in 1916. Stalin liked to claim the credit for double-tracking the trans-Siberian completely, but in fact some substantial lengths of single line remained east of Irkutsk into Khruschev's time. J P Pearson noted a lot of double-track in use and under construction in 1913. By the mid-1970s three-quarters of the railway (starting from the European end) had been electrified. A second trans-Siberian railway, further to the north and away from the Chinese border, is now under construction. From 1912 until their defeat in 1945 the Japanese operated a connecting route leading via Manchuria and what is now Korea to Pusan, a port that was specially convenient for travellers to Japan. It was all an incredible feat and, for anyone who travelled it, well worth writing about.

Below and Right:
The traditional magnificence of Moscow stations.

Both the history of and journeys on the trans-Siberian railway are well documented in Harmon Tupper's definitive account, *To The Great Ocean* (Secker & Warburg, 1965). His accounts of journeying in Siberia begin with travelling conditions in pre-railway days. The months it then took, the 'bugs,' the bad food and the unspeakable accommodation make gruesome reading. But soon after the line was opened both the Russian Government and the Wagons-Lits Company entered the fray with de-luxe trains. The Church Car that legend says was provided in fact only offered static religious sustenance for railwaymen at places along the line, while the car with baths very often did not get put on. Wagons-Lits showed some very super-special cars for this run at the Paris Exhibition of 1900, but in the end decided not to submit any but their ordinary ones to the tender mercies of Siberian conditions. Tupper includes snippets from the writings of many pre-1914 travellers. One thing has not changed – the service is highly variable from fairly good to downright awful.

A man called J P Pearson, who wrote about his worldwide travels in his monumental million-word three-volume *Railways And Scenery* (Cassell, 1932), travelled across the USSR in 1913 when things had settled down. He left Moscow at 38 seconds past 9.09 am on 30 July, calling (for example, in case you are interested) at Omsk from 3.31.12 pm to 3.49.16 pm, when 4–6–0 No 230 was replaced by No 203. Detailed stopping or passing times at most stations over most of the journey, even in the small hours, were recorded to the nearest second. His destination was Japan, so he changed at Changchun, arriving 41 minutes 2 seconds behind schedule, he reports, although very worried about his luggage at the time. He then took the Japanese controlled route through Manchuria and Korea to Pusan. Some very superior trains (of which Pearson speaks highly) ran on this line; they had been obtained regardless of cost from Pullman of the USA. They even continued running after their connections with Europe (and, hence, their entire *raison d'être*) had ceased, as Henry Carew found when he joined one almost by chance at Pyongyang.

His account (published in *The Railway Magazine* during 1952), tells of what might be called the ultimate in rail travel comfort, as the following extract indicates. . . .

I had a personal experience of the luxury service towards the end of 1916. Business took me from Japan to Korea and as far north as the town now known as Pyongyang. It was not a very pleasant place in the bitterly cold weather of a Korean November, and I was not sorry when my work came to an end. While looking up a train to take me to Pusan, on the first stage of my journey back to Tokyo, I suddenly remembered it was a Friday, the one day of the week when the special train was still running. The officials at the station pointed out that I could travel just as comfortably by the ordinary daily train at substantially less expense, and get

in about five more hours in transit for my money. Moreover, my request to travel on the express meant digging out special tickets which they hardly ever used and consequently knew very little about. However, I insisted, and finally had my way.

Just before 3 pm, and sharp on time the train rolled smoothly into the platform and came to a dignified stop. It was headed by a great Pacific locomotive, cleaned and polished to exhibition standard, and followed by long, sleek carriages finished in dark green and gold. Hovering round it were a large number of young Japanese attendants in smart uniforms. As there were some minutes to spare, I walked the length of the train along the platform and it was only then I realized that I was the only passenger. The time of departure approached and the station-master stepped out of his office, came up to me and saluted, and asked if I would kindly entrain. He was followed by the Chef-de-Train, who also saluted and escorted me to the door of my sleeping car. A boy then led me down a softly-carpeted corridor and ushered me into a beautifully-furnished compartment, which he informed me was my sitting room, and indicated that the adjoining one was my bedroom; then he bowed low and left me. There was a deep and melodious note from the whistle, an orgy of saluting between the station and the train staff, and then we drew smoothly out.

Tea appeared to be indicated so I strolled along more carpeted corridors until I reached

the dining car, which I found to be a flawless symphony of ivory white ceiling, large plate-glass windows, beautiful panelling, and perfect table appointments. Here I had a choice of 24 seats, with four waiters to serve me with tea, and there was no scrimping in any way, everything was in full working order – light, heating, and flowers on all the tables. I asked the head waiter, a little facetiously I fear, if there was sufficient food to see us through to Pusan and he replied in all seriousness that there should be enough. Questioned further, he volunteered the amazing information that on every trip they stocked up with full rations for 48 passengers, and that the bulk of this was discarded at the end of the journey and replaced with fresh provisions. It was magnificent but hardly economic!

Night was closing in and the outlook became more dismal than ever. The attendant entered softly, drew down the curtains and turned on several cunningly-placed lights, examined the thermostat to see if the temperature was right, asked if there was anything which I wanted, and then withdrew. The train ran on smoothly and almost in silence, so beautifully was it sprung and insulated from all outside influence. A tap at the door and the Chef-de-Train presented himself. 'Is everything quite all right sir? Please let me know if there is anything you wish attended to. We reach Keijo (Seoul) at nine o'clock, and Pusan at seven tomorrow morning.' Then came the head waiter, complete with menu, to ask at what time I would

like my dinner. Would the *table d'hôte* be satisfactory, or would I like something cooked specially? Perhaps I would like a cocktail and *hors d'oeuvre* served in my room first? That important preliminary having been attended to by two waiters and with much ceremony, I made my way to the dining car.

The restaurant had been transformed. Blinds had all been drawn down and the place was a blaze of light with the added touch of rose-shaded lamps on each table. The dinner was perfectly cooked and served and the incongruity forced itself on me. Instead of running empty through the wilds of a desolate country like Korea the train should have been on its way, crowded with well-dressed passengers, to the Riviera, or to one of the romantic capitals of Southern Europe.

And now two of my attendants came along and proceeded to make up a most comfortable bed in the adjoining room, in which they invited me to take my rest. As this was the first, and quite probably the last, time on which I should ever enjoy the great thrill of having a special train all to myself (and what a train!), it seemed a pity to spend several hours of the time in sleep, but I had to think of the feelings of the staff, who would probably consider it incumbent on them to stay up until I had retired.

We reached the Pusan pier sharp at 7 am, after they had served me with an early breakfast in the dining car, and I was bowed off the train in great style by the entire staff.

Extreme right:
Soviet Railways' latest type of electric express train.

Below:
The Siberian scene viewed from a window of the 'Russia' express.

On the other hand, Somerset Maugham, in a short story called 'Mr Harrington's Washing,' described briefly but with shattering vividness a war-time journey (in fact based on his own experience) on the 'Trans-Siberian' proper, just as the revolution got into its stride. Mr Harrington, expostulating about lawless and uncivilized behavior, ended up (of course) just as dead as several other travellers who hadn't bothered to complain first. It is not made quite clear why Maugham was sent that way when he could perfectly well have travelled direct via Norway, Sweden and what is now Finland, as did author Arthur Ransome (famous for the 'Swallows and Amazons' children's books), who was also in Russia at that time. Ransome got away complete with spoils of war in the form of Trotsky's secretary, whom he later married – but the only trans-Siberian journey mentioned in his books is much later when the father of the 'Swallows' – Com-

mander Walker, RN – travels home from China that way and unexpectedly finds his children sailing into Flushing Harbor (*We Didn't Mean To Go To Sea*). However, it is unlikely that serving British naval officers could travel through Russia in the 1930s.

Some time had to elapse after the revolution before the line was available again to voluntary travellers although many 'political' prisoners enjoyed the line as far as Siberia in the years immediately after the revolution.

Peter Fleming, elder brother of Ian Fleming, journeyed far and wide in the USSR. Some people have all the luck, because his trans-Siberian train became seriously derailed near Chita in 1933 – the dining car and his sleeper turned over on their sides – thereby distracting the staff's attention (this was the period when station masters got shot for things like that). Fleming took the opportunity to use his camera and, hence,

those fascinating photographs published in *One's Company* (Jonathan Cape, 1934). The pictures show the pre-war Wagons-Lits cars, confiscated without compensation by the Bolsheviks in 1918.

Regarding photographs (and their confiscation), photography inside the USSR has always been a problem, and still is today. If one is caught taking photographs without permission *all* one's films are confiscated. Fleming got away with it by sitting on the films he had exposed, while allowing (under great protest) the officials to find and confiscate one containing pictures of his grandmother. It is rather grim to think that, after the book was published, these men would no doubt have been purged.

One well-known photographer, Ron Ziel, anxious in 1970 to record the superb class P-36 steam 4–8–4s, then still running east of Baikal, succeeded by using a huge press camera, built like a battleship and taking 4 × 5 inch plates. After setting this up on the platform he then accosted the most important-looking policeman and requested using his one memorized Russian phrase 'Please get the platform cleared, I wish to photograph the train.' Ziel came back with some wonderful pictures offered to us in *Twilight of World Steam* (Grosset & Dunlap, 1973). His account of taking them was published in *Trains Magazine* in July 1971. His behavior did result in his being banned from further excursions into the Soviet Union.

Christopher Portway is the only traveller of recent years who made it to Vladivostok, the Pacific terminus of the 'Russia.' Foreigners are now diverted on to the Nakhodka branch, changing at Khabarovsk, because Vladivostok is a naval base and off-limits to visitors. Portway gave his Intourist 'guide' the slip at Khabarovsk and made it to Vladivostok and back. His absence without leave from the hotel was reported, but

A Soviet Railways' class VL23 electric locomotive hauls a train into Kursk station in Moscow in 1959.

Intourist was hampered in its interrogation by having to maintain a posture of polite curiosity.

Eric Newby, who has lately written a whole book (*The Great Red Train Ride*) on the subject, also had trouble with Intourist's ambiguous role – he refers to them throughout as 'The Agency.' He did not really enjoy the journey but more because of a general sense of totalitarian oppressiveness than any real discomfort. After all, he had served his time before the mast in windjammers as well as travelling down the Ganges in a rowing boat. Even so, his account explains why some travellers enjoy themselves and others do not. He stopped off quite often and so kept changing one 'Russia' for another; one car attendant or one dining car crew would like foreigners and bother – others did not. Incidentally, around 16 'Russia' trains would be moving across the land at any one time, involving approximately 25 different crews.

Sympathizing with this attitude in his review of that book was Paul Theroux who in his best-seller *The Great Railway Bazaar*, (Penguin Books, 1974), found the 'Russia' a bit tedious to travel back on after he had travelled out east via Turkey, Iran, India and Vietnam. The catalog of writings on the 'Russia' is endless but one theme runs through them all – the pleasure of contacts with Soviet fellow-travellers, who generally feel freer to hob-nob with foreigners on trains than they do in other situations in the Soviet Union. J P Pearson was the only writer who evidently found a lot of the scenery interesting, and in his dry way recalls the excitement of seeing a virgin country being settled for the very first time. Modern writers however tend to dwell on how dreary most of the landscape is.

One traveller who enjoyed himself with huge gusto was Rogers Whitaker; he describes it very wittily in *All Aboard With E M Frimbo*, (Andre Deutsch, 1974 – written in conjunction with Anthony Hiss). His little group had a lovely Intourist lady to look after them, who brooked no nonsense with the huge useless menus (almost everything crossed off) – just insisted that they all had large helpings of caviar for breakfast. 'The caviar is fresh Caspian Sea caviar, not the salted stuff we are used to in the USA,' he says.

But of all these and many more, the writer's favorite for romance and effect is that of John Price (Editor of Cook's timetable), who describes the 'Russia' and its associated trains each month in the following style:

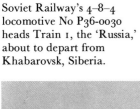

Soviet Railway's 4–8–4 locomotive No P36-0030 heads Train 1, the 'Russia,' about to depart from Khabarovsk, Siberia.

Table 878   MOSKVA - IRKUTSK - KHABAROVSK - NAKHODKA

TRANS-SIBERIAN RAILWAY

12 fast	2 fast	10 fast	km		Moscow Time		1 fast	9 fast	11 fast	Time (Z)
N 2035	**B** 1000	**D** 1440	0	dep.	**Moskva** (Yaroslavski)	arr.	**B** 1220	**D** 5 40	**D** 6 30	0
1st day	*1st day*	*1st day*					*9th day*	*4th day*	*4th day*	
1219 / 1234	1 16 / 1 34	6 23 / 6 46	957	arr. / dep.	Kirov	dep. / arr.	2121 / 2106	1428 / 1413	1452 / 1437	1 2
2nd day	*2nd day*	*2nd day*							*3rd day*	
3 17 / 3 32	1549 / 1604	2028 / 2045	1818	arr. / dep.	**Sverdlovsk**	dep. / arr.	7 08 / 6 48	2353 / 2338	2340 / 2325	3
3rd day							*8th day*		*2nd day*	
1730 / 1748	6 00 / 6 31	1100 / 1115	2716	arr. / dep.	Omsk	dep. / arr.	1612 / 1557	9 07 / 8 50	9 35 / 9 20	
	3rd day	*3rd day*					*7th day*	*3rd day*		
3 57 / 4 35	1706 / 1726	2155 / 2215	3343	arr. / dep.	Novosibirsk	dep. / arr.	6 45 / 6 25	2158 / 2142	2300 / 2245	4
4th day									*1st day*	
1855	7 00 / 7 16	1158 / 1213	4104	arr. / dep.	Krasnoyarsk	dep. / arr.	1635 / 1620	8 05 / 7 44	9 00	
	4th day	*4th day*					*6th day*	*2nd day*		
..	2 46 / 2 51	8 20	5184	arr. / dep.	**Irkutsk**	dep. / arr.	2100 / 2050	1208	..	4
	5th day	*5th day*						*1st day*		
..	1114 / 1132	..	5647	arr. / dep.	Ulan Ude	dep. / arr.	1245 / 1228	..	..	5
							5th day			
..	2126 / 2140	..	6204	arr. / dep.	Chita	dep. / arr.	1 45 / 1 25	..	..	6
..	2056 / 2111	..	7313	arr. / dep.	Skovorodino	dep. / arr.	1 38 / 1 23	..	..	
	6th day						*4th day*			
..	4 35	..	8531	arr. / dep.	Khabarovsk	dep. / arr.	7 55 / 7 30	..	..	
	8th day c 4 55						*c erd day / c 3rd day*			
..	1905	..	9297	arr.	**Vladivostok**	dep.	1650	..	..	7
	8th day c						*c 2nd day*			

Passengers travelling to Japan must change at Khabarovsk (staying overnight westbound) and continue by fast train 3/4:

	4 AG		km				FG			
..	8th day c 1825	..	8531	dep.	Khabarovsk	arr.	1110 c 2nd day	..	..	7
..	9th day c 9 40	..	9441	arr.	Nakhodka	dep.	2000 c 1st day	..	..	7

Further details are given in *The Great Siberian Route* published twice yearly by Intourist, 292 Regent Street, London W1R 7PO.
A—Runs only on day prior to sailings from Nakhodka to Japan shown in Table **1467**.
B—RUSSIA—Runs daily, Sleeping car, Soft and hard cars and   Moskva–Vladivostok and v.v.
D—BAIKAL—Runs daily June to Sept., with soft and hard cars and restaurant car Moskva–Irkutsk and v.v.
F—Runs only on arrival dates of steamers from Japan (Table **1467**).
G—Sleeping car, hard cars and restaurant car Khabarovsk–Nakhodka and v.v.
N—YENISEI—Soft and hard cars and restaurant car Moskva–Krasnoyarsk and v.v.
Z—Local Time differs from Moscow Time by the number of hours shown.
c—Local Time (seven hours ahead of Moscow Time).   —The railway station at Nakhodka Port is named Tikhookeanskaya.

The Soviet Railways' class E 0–10–0 steam locomotives were once the world's most numerous type but are now reduced to a few survivors used for shunting and trip work.

Scandinavia

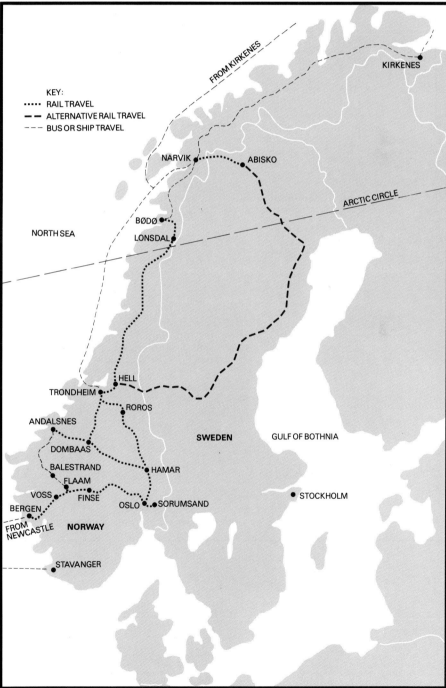

KEY:
...... RAIL TRAVEL
— — ALTERNATIVE RAIL TRAVEL
– – BUS OR SHIP TRAVEL

FROM KIRKENES

KIRKENES

NARVIK   ABISKO

ARCTIC CIRCLE

NORTH SEA

BØDØ

LONSDAL

HELL

TRONDHEIM

ROROS

ANDALSNES

DOMBAAS   SWEDEN   GULF OF BOTHNIA

BALESTRAND
FLAAM   HAMAR

VOSS   FINSE   STOCKHOLM

BERGEN   OSLO   SORUMSAND

FROM   NORWAY
NEWCASTLE

STAVANGER

The railway systems of Scandinavia are not only pleasantly different from railways elsewhere but also from each other. All are well worth a visit and, indeed, train travel in Scandinavia is a real treat – the trains have an edge on most of the rest of the world, being particularly clean and spacious, efficiently run as well as value for money. Of the Scandinavian countries Norway is the one that offers the most spectacular rides, because of its mountains.

The only through cars to run to Norway from outside Scandinavia are (inevitably) from Moscow via Berlin, with not only the usual bogie-changing but a train-ferry ride as well. Even these only run once a week in summer only. Oslo is easily reached, of course, by train (using at least two train ferries and at least one of Denmark's fabulous over-sea bridges), changing at Copenhagen; Copenhagen is reachable direct from most European countries. But surely one of the greatest seafaring nations of the world is more appropriately reached by a sea crossing, which brings us, oddly enough, to the only *train* to leave a non-Scandinavian capital regularly with passengers bound for Norway. . . .

Route 12 Where the Sun Never Sets

Time was when 'The Norseman' rolled down the East Coast Main Line (see Route 1) from London, bound for a quayside called Tyne Commission Quay at the mouth of the River Tyne. Then, after a strange and surprisingly long journey through dockland sidings, the train would draw up alongside one of the Bergen Line's magnificent ships.

Today the visitor to Norway must take a connecting bus from Newcastle to the dockyard but no doubt the superb Smorgasbrød 'help-yourself' meals on the ship are as good as ever they were. Bergen is reached the next afternoon. Next morning, well fortified by one of those amazing Norse breakfasts, the visitor is introduced to the Norske Statsbaner (Norwegian State Railways) by its most famous line, the Bergen-Oslo Railway. Starting just before the turn of the century, it took 10 years of traumatic toil to connect Bergen with what was then the capital of a newly independent country; the climate in a land where the *permanent* snow-line is only 2500ft above sea level was the worst enemy. Construction gangs working in the mountains during the winter were cut off for months at a time.

It is now an eight-hour electric journey for 300 miles over the top to Oslo (it was 11 hours 50 minutes in steam days but the electric trains have the advantage of various improvements to cut off corners as well as faster running). A second great 4–8–0 used to be needed for the climb from Voss, at more or less sea level, to over 4000ft altitude at Finse, where snow reaches the eaves of the station buildings in winter and the trains run in long tunnels of snow-sheds. Electrification has meant some amelioration of the rather severe pattern of train service here, which also applied to other main-line sectors, Oslo to Bergen, Stavanger and Trondheim, *viz*, one day train with diner and one night train with sleepers.

Oslo is reached in nice time to settle in for the night; a recommendation is the great hotel at Holmenkollen, on the famous ski mountain high above the city, which one reaches by a strange little line that can never quite make up its mind whether it is an underground railroad, a mountain railway, or a streetcar line. Nansen's ship *Fram* is on view here, set as fast in concrete as she ever was in polar ice; there is also a rather fine folk museum, which has full-sized replicas of Norse houses down the ages from very, very early times. One can get a steam 'fix' not far away at Sørumsand, a station on the Oslo-Stockholm main line. The line is a 2½-mile long surviving stretch of the Holandsbane, a 2ft 5½in gauge branch. Two of the original 2–6–2Ts do the honors.

The Norwegian State Railway Museum is 80 miles north of Oslo at Hamar on the way to Trondheim, which is our next destination. Many full-size locomotives are preserved in the museum.

There is also a short 2ft gauge line which offers live operation. If one stops off at Hamar, good 'banemanship' ('bane' is Norwegian for railway) would make one be quite certain that he had accommodation reserved on from Hamar – there is always a slight question mark over joining trains (which are liable to be full) at an intermediate station for a long journey. In fact two routes, both carrying through trains, lead to Trondheim, the electric main line direct (the 'Dovre-bane') and the original roundabout once-narrow-gauge route via Roros. The choice would depend on how much time the traveller had; it seems the slower route would involve an extra night, probably at Hamar, because the Roros route through train leaves at 1035, rather early to have completed a tour of the museum. The 'Dovre Express' leaves Hamar at 1641 and runs into Trondheim (in broad daylight if it is anywhere near midsummer) at 2210.

The Norlandsbane which leads on north from Trondheim another 456 miles to Bødø, has still the two-trains-daily pattern of service, one by day and one by night; the night train (complete with sleeping cars) makes a good connection with the 'Dovre Express.' Beyond Mo-i-Rana, at breakfast time next morning (a breakfast car is included in the set), the Arctic Circle is crossed – in mid-summer no more sunsets, in mid-winter no more sunrises! The scenery has its own wild beauty to match the remoteness of the location; one is 800 miles from Oslo when Bødø is reached at 11 o'clock. This line, incidentally, was completed during the 1960s.

This is still not the end of Norwegian railways and, if ever last was not least, the famous iron-ore railway leading to the port of Narvik is such a case. However, to reach Narvik by train from Bødø one has to go back 725 miles and change at Hell (!); then after a further two changes in

A Norwegian State Railways' 4–8–0 locomotive leads the southbound Norlandsbane train at Londsdal, south of Bødø.

Above:
The iron-ore quays at
Narvik, Norway.

Top:
A Norwegian State
Railways' train prepares to
leave Bergen station in
steam days.

Sweden (at Ange and Boden), Norwegian rails are reached again two days later. May one be forgiven for putting forward the $7\frac{1}{2}$-hour bus ride as an alternative, especially as it is a most enjoyable alternative with fabulous mountain roads and tiny car ferries (on which the bus has priority)? One of these fjord crossings is quite long and lunch is served on board. The bus in fact connects with the train at Fauske, 35 miles short of Bødø.

Narvik is not a place to linger in; fortunately there is a good connection (20 minutes) with the last passenger train of the day over the Ofotenbane iron-ore line to the Swedish Lapland tourist station of Abisko. This is a government-run establishment alongside an immense and beautiful lake, and it offers the complete spectrum of accommodation from rooms with a private bathroom to bunk-house. It is also specially appropriate to this book in that it has (a) its own railway station and (b) no road leading to it. The

hotel part is notable for a *north*-facing sun verandah, to observe the sun as it dips towards (but never reaches) the horizon at midnight. For the train buff, superb rod-drive three-unit electric locomotives (of 1–D + D + D–1 wheel arrangement) go roaring by every 30 minutes or so, hauling immense iron-ore trains.

Back at Narvik, since there are 640 miles of Norway left, one might take the Nord-Norge bus service, spending two nights en route, to Kirkenes, near the *Soviet* border, and crossing the 70° parallel of latitude in the process. Return to Trondheim would be by one of the famous daily *Hurtig-rute* ('Express route') steamers; Trondheim is reached, via the famous North Cape, in the early morning of the fifth day on board, after an unforgettable (in the nicest sense) voyage. Of course, one could return by train from Abisko to Oslo via Stockholm or even take a short connecting trip by steamer from Narvik and pick up the *Hurtig-rute* at Solvaer.

Left:
A Norwegian State Railways' passenger train on the Bergen-Oslo Railway near Finse. Note the extensive snow-sheds.
Below:
Two 4–8–0s of the Norwegian State Railways climb out of Voss with a Bergen-Oslo express.

Returning from Trondheim, one should proceed south on the main line to Dombaas, and then experience Norwegian branch line travel on the exciting Andalsnes branch, the Rauma-bane. From Andalsnes, connecting buses can be taken via Hellesylt and some fantastic roads (with more little ferries) to Balestrand on the Sogne Fjord. The objective is a place on the opposite shore called Flaam (some of the trips across involve changing steamers in mid-fjord), whence runs an amazing piece of railway construction. The line leads up to Myrdal, a station high up above on the Oslo-Bergen railway, only six miles away horizontally, but almost $\frac{3}{4}$-mile up measured vertically. Somehow a $12\frac{1}{2}$-mile alignment has been squeezed into the space, by means of incredible convolutions. From Myrdal, trains are available both to Bergen and Oslo, both places from which it is convenient but rather sad to bid goodbye to Norway and her fascinating transport systems.

South America

PANAMA CANAL
CARACAS
VENEZUELA
GUYANA
SURINAM
FRENCH GUIANA
MEDELLIN
PORTO BERRIO
ARMENIA
BOGOTA
CALI
GIRARDOT
COLOMBIA
SAN LORENZO
QUITO
DURAN
SIBAMBE
CUENCA
GUAYAQUIL
R. AMAZON
SAN LUIZ
RECIFE
PERU
CERRO DE PASCO
OROYA
LIMA
HUANCAYO
CALLAO
QUILLABAMBA
MACCHU – PICCHU
CUZCO
HUANCAVELICA
BRAZIL
SAN SALVADOR
LAKE TITICACA
LA PAZ
ORURO
COCHABAMBA
SUCRE
POTOSI
IQUIQUE
UYUNI
BRAZILIA
ANTOFAGASTA
PARAGUAY
SAO PAOLO
RIO DE JANEIRO
SERRA DE MAR INCLINES
ASCUNION
SANTOS
TUCUMAN
ENCARNACION
POSADOS
TUBARAO
CORDOBA
SALTO
VAL PARAISO
MENDOZA
CONCORDIA
PAYSANDU
PASO DE LOS TOROS
SANTIAGO
URUGUAY
MONTEVIDEO
ARGENTINA
BUENOS AIRES
CHILE
BAHIA BLANCA
SAN CARLOS DE BRRILOCHE
PACIFIC OCEAN

0   SCALE   500 MILES

RIO TURBIO MINES   RIO GALLEGOS

Early development of railways in this vast and still partly unexplored continent was influenced chiefly by the needs of the export trades. Lines were first constructed into the interior from ports, to carry agricultural produce or minerals for shipment to Europe or North America, and in most cases it was British interests which promoted and financed them. It was not until late in the 19th century that this piecemeal pattern of individual railways began to be turned, by the construction of linking lines, into any sort of national network; and it was only in Argentina and Chile, and to a lesser extent in Brazil and Uruguay, that any kind of coherent nation- or region-wide system really evolved. In much the same way, the physical equipment of the railways, and even their gauges, were influenced at the start by local and not national considerations.

Government policies were slow to change this state of affairs. During the 19th century, governments had no choice in the matter; they had no resources to build railways themselves, and indeed were more inclined to encourage railway-building on any terms which enhanced national economic development rather than to want to do anything to influence and so retard the work of foreign capital. Quite apart from this, South American governments had the deserved reputation at this time of being unstable. But by the middle of the 20th century things had changed; nearly all the railways had, for instance, been nationalized, and foreign capital no longer had its original 'stranglehold' on the national transport arteries. Politicians were thereby much pleased; but any practical differences took longer to appear. Political instability remained endemic; the massive resources needed to carry out the modernization and redevelopment of the railways could scarcely be found. Some impressive progress has been made here and there; but the general picture remains one of a great variety of types of equipment, of gauge, and an often inconvenient route pattern.

Nowadays South American passenger trains vary from air-conditioned luxury to spartan wood-slat seats; from thrice-daily expresses to one mixed train a week; and sweating overcrowded rush-hour suburban runs to the bitter cold of the high Andean desert. Life is supported on the way, of course; whether by the cold meat and rice emerging from the primitive kitchens of Bolivian or Paraguayan dining cars, to steak and wine in Chile and Argentina. Fares are generally very cheap, and some international rail passes are available to foreign visitors.

Northern South America offers thin fare to the railway traveller. Although Guyana once boasted the first railway on the South American mainland, no public railways now exist there or in neighboring Surinam or French Guiana. Venezuela possesses only one short standard-gauge line, first, and so far only, flower of a planned second-generation national railway system, the first having been closed down during the first flush of infatuation with the automobile. Colombia's national railway network has continued to expand, though slowly, and now comprises some 2200 miles of 3ft gauge track linking the large cities of the central provinces with a main line paralleling the great Magdalena River.

Further south, the main line of Ecuador's 3ft 6in gauge railway runs 288 miles from Duran, across the river from the main port of Guayaquil, to Quito, the cool Andean capital. Later government-built extensions added the Quito-San Lorenzo and Sibambe-Cuenca lines to complete the system. Peruvian railways consist of two distinct systems, each standard gauge with 3ft

The highest rails on earth: the mine spur at La Cima on the Central Railway of Peru at an altitude of 15,806ft.

gauge feeders, totalling only 1129 route-miles. The Central Railway links Callao port through Lima, the capital, with Cerro de Pasco, Oroya and Huancayo in the high Andes. The Southern Railway strikes inland from the twin ports of Mollendo and Matarani, via Arequipa to Puno on Lake Titicaca, and Cuzco, the ancient Inca capital. Huancayo and Cuzco are each the starting point of a 3ft gauge railway, running respectively south to Huancavelica and north to Quillabamba, the latter line busy with the tourist trade to the world-famous 'Lost City' of the Incas at Macchu-Picchu.

The Bolivian railway system totals 2240 route-miles of meter-gauge line. The western system, running on the altiplano at an average altitude of some 11,000ft, accounts for 1384 miles; the remaining 856 miles radiate from Santa Cruz, in the humid and dusty eastern lowlands. The two sections are still unconnected, except by way of a 400-mile detour through Argentina.

Chile is shaped on the map not so much like a sausage, more like a length of string. Its railway system is therefore necessarily laid out rather like a snake's skeleton, or rather the skeleton of two snakes sharing the same head. This head is at Valparaiso, the main port half-way along the length of the country. From nearby Calera the northern system, of meter gauge, runs parallel to the coast for 1160 miles to Iquique, throwing off several branches and an important secondary route from Antofagasta inland to connect with Bolivia. The passenger service on this lengthy main line consists of two trains a week, which traverse desert landscapes where no rain has fallen in living memory. In stark contrast, the broad-gauge (5ft 6in) southern system, commencing at Valparaiso and serving the capital city of Santiago, has a busy and partly electrified

main line running 782 miles southwards to Puerto Montt, again with numerous branches, all in fertile and beautiful country.

When 80 percent of Argentina's railways were operated by British companies, they formed one of the world's most efficient and comprehensive systems, and certainly far the best in South America. Since nationalization in 1949, whether or not for that reason, (though certainly Argentine politics had something to do with it), the railways became seriously neglected, maintenance deteriorated, and replacement of rolling stock fell into arrears. The fiercely competitive days of the late 19th century had left a legacy of three gauges, thousands of route-miles of now redundant tracks, and a multitude of locomotive and rolling stock designs. Partial modernization has resulted in diesel-hauled trains (some now fairly ancient) still having to struggle along on sub-standard permanent track to slow schedules.

Uruguay's compact standard-gauge railway system radiates from Montevideo, the capital and main port, along 1850 miles of line over which new Ganz railcars and older diesel-hauled trains operate rather sparse services. Speeds are slow but riding generally smooth, and the whole operation moderately well-run. A small pocket of steam locomotives lingers in the Paysandu and Salto areas.

The only public railway in Paraguay is standard-gauge and runs for 234 miles southward from the capital, Asuncion, to Encarnacion on the Parana River, connecting there with a train ferry linking with an Argentine standard-gauge railway which eventually, by means of another train ferry several hundred miles further on, gets to Buenos Aires. A thrice-weekly mixed train, operated by elderly woodburning steam locomotives, moves the traffic (though not much

A class 57 2–6–0 hauls a branch line train to Traiguen on the broad-gauge system which serves the southern part of Chile.

meaning can be read any longer into the words 'moves' or 'traffic') in an astonishing assortment of rolling stock. But for the hardened enthusiast, a Paraguayan train journey is one of the more highly rated railway experiences. From time to time plans are announced to electrify, and presumably to modernize in other ways, this line, but nothing has yet actually happened so far.

Brazilian railways had a similar history to Argentina's. But after a period of neglect almost as complete, reconstruction and indeed extension has been pressed forward energetically since the late 1950s. The standard Brazilian gauge is one meter, though several thousand miles of 5ft 3in line also exist, centered at Rio de Janeiro and São Paulo. Trains on both gauges are comfortable but slow, and while services between the large urban complexes are good, this is not so over the greater part of the country. But then, the greater

part of Brazil consists of the largest untamed wilderness on earth.

So much for a thumbnail history of a continent's railway system. The area which they cover is so vast, the railways so disconnected, and the trains in general so slow and infrequent that it is hardly possible to conceive of any tourist ever actually making the journey we are about to describe; one would need many months to do it properly, to stop along the way and absorb something of the quite different styles of life and landscape. Serious long-distance travellers in South America fly, or if possible go by bus, over most of the itinerary. So in this chapter we must say, even more firmly than usual, that we are not seriously proposing a practical undertaking; but even so, any traveller choosing any part of the theoretically possible route will be having a rare and rewarding experience.

Left:
A class 57 2–6–0 crosses the mile-long bridge at Bio-Bio, Chile, with a freight bound for Concepcion.

Below:
A Bolivian mixed train from Rio Mulato to Potosi at Yura is headed by 4–8–2 No 811.

Route 13
The Highest
Rails of All

It may be doubted whether anybody has ever actually travelled all the way from northern Colombia to southern Chile, down the whole length of the Andes, then swung back north to come close to encircling the whole of South America through Argentina, Uruguay, and Brazil. However, this is the journey about to be described; and maybe the description will prod somebody into doing it. About half the distance is possible by rail, and where trains exist they shall be used; alternatively, lake, river, or coastal steamers, or buses, (in that order of permissibility only). Airplanes are prohibited. Following the same absolutism, the journey shall start at Santa Marta, the northernmost point in South America served by rail, regardless of the fact that any person arriving in Columbia from abroad will almost certainly be set down first at the capital, Bogota, some 500 miles to the south.

However, the first lap, from Santa Marta to Bogota itself, is an untypically easy one, in that it can be covered in quite a comfortable, if a not very fast, daily train. The first two-thirds of the distance, along the level and near the broad Magdalena River (still plied by stern-wheelers) were actually built fairly recently, in the 1950s; trackage in the mountain districts south of Puerto Berrio is older. Bogota, on the high and cool Sabana plateau, is a well-sited city rather spoiled by some intractable social and political problems, so one is unlikely to want to linger; the way to the south lies through Cali. This could theoretically be reached by rail from Santa Marta, leaving the main line at Puerto Berrio and passing through the third city of Colombia, Medellin: however, half the Medellin to Cali line does not actually operate. So the practical route is train from

Bogota to Girardot, bus from Girardot to Armenia over the 11,000ft Quindio Pass, and then again train from Armenia to Cali. (Even more practical, and a one-day journey, but disallowed under the rules, is bus throughout.) However, the Colombian railways offer much of interest; there are still some survivors here and there of the old steam fleet, which once included some rare articulated types to cope with the very difficult curves and grades, and mountaineering curiosities like Esperanza station on the Bogota-Girardot line, which never sees a train unless the locomotive is pushing at the back, since it is situated on the center leg of a double zig-zag.

From Cali to Quito in Ecuador, some 300 miles, there is little alternative but to take the second of what will become a long series of Andean buses. A third of the distance could perhaps be covered by train, with a line running from each end towards the border, but trains on these sections are rather remote and unreliable.

South of Quito, however, on the next leg of 288 miles, the famous Guayaquil & Quito line is a very practical travel possibility indeed, and a remarkable one. The schedule offers a fast diesel railcar three days a week, doing the run in 10 hours; this may not sound fast, but with many obstacles en route it is actually a horn-blaring, dust-raising, helter-skelter rush. An alternative is to use the mixed train, trundling gently along the 11,000ft high plateau under Cotopaxi to an overnight stop at Riobamba. Next day, with 20,000ft Chimborazo the presiding mountain, one descends to the coastal plains along the famous Devil's Nose switchbacks above Sibambe, dropping 5000ft in 24 miles with a ruling gradient of 1 in 19 – and more to the point, a very good

A Baldwin 2–8–2 crosses the Magdalena River Bridge at Girardot, Colombia.

chance of seeing and being hauled by some well-maintained steam locomotives which are still at work on this very dramatic section. The final length to Duran and Guayaquil is through sugarcane fields and mango groves, across the coastal plain.

The next leg, Guayaquil to Lima in Peru, is, under the rules, a bus marathon; something over 36 hours of continuous progress, not counting an easy start in the overnight steamer to Puerto Bolivar. But recovery pauses at various towns en route, all devoid of railways (except for a few industrial short lines) are possible and permissible. Be it said at this point that roads are, in these latitudes, only marginally more common than railways. The road map of Ecuador and northern Peru is sketchy in the extreme, with basically only one north-south link; and then for the three thousand miles across Amazonia to the Atlantic coast, there is only one other north-south highway. Our snorting bus is a very rare and recent phenomenon.

The Central Railway of Peru, built between 1870 and 1893 by the American, Henry Meiggs, is certainly one of the seven wonders of the railway world. It runs from the port of Callao, through Lima, the capital city, up and over the main

Above:
Ecuador's 3ft 6in gauge Guayaquil & Quito Railway. Here a Baldwin 2–8–0 shunts at Quito.

Center left:
Ecuador's Guayaquil & Quito Railway climbs the Devil's Nose. Even though switchbacks are used, the gradient is as steep as 1 in 18.

Andes chain to Oroya and Huancayo. An important standard-gauge branch runs from Oroya to the coppermining center of Cerro de Pasco and, as mentioned, a 3ft gauge extension runs from Huancayo to Huancavelica. The main line is barely over 200 miles long but in the 99 miles from Lima to the summit in the Galera tunnel it passes through 13 reversing stations and 66 tunnels, across 59 viaducts, and runs along miles of vertiginous mountain ledges. The main passenger train now runs only three days a week, and is of course diesel-hauled but on average during the main climb taking some $4\frac{1}{2}$ hours, ascends over 50 feet per minute. The train includes, of course, a dining car, and carries supplies of oxygen for passengers overcome by mountain sickness, together with an attendant to administer it. For years steam ruled unchallenged in these mountains, since no diesel could function properly over such a range of altitudes; finally General Motors developed a special turbocharger to force enough oxygen into the cylinders, and that was that. Some steam however, still survives on the 3ft gauge and perhaps also on the Cerro de Pasco line.

One must not weaken and take to the air for the next hop; it must instead be another bus epic, three days along the Andean back roads to Cuzco. But then there is another gap in the road system, one strangely enough filled by the other Peruvian narrow-gauge line from Cuzco to Quillabamba. Even apart from the considerable railway interest of making a detour along this still partly steam-worked branch, it is an essential part of any South American tour since it is the only way to get to the fabled ruins of Macchu-Picchu. One can do the journey out-and-back in a day by railcar, or by staying overnight in the hotel nearby, by steam-hauled mixed train. From the ancient city's summit, the views are unforgettable, with stone staircases, temples and terraces, clinging in breathtaking fashion to a razor-backed high ridge between two mountain peaks. White llamas graze the lawns, and tourists browse also.

The other railway at Cuzco, the Southern of Peru, is a much longer outfit than the Central, with some 500 miles of track. The main line runs from Cuzco through Juliaca to the southern capital of Arequipa and the port of Mollendo; there is a branch from Juliaca to the highest navigable waters in the world, 12,650ft high Lake Titicaca at Puno. Although it reaches heights scarcely less than the Central, and has ruling gradients that are worse (1 in 18 instead of 1 in 22, all adhesion-worked), the Southern is not so spectacular for its scenery or its engineering.

One can now leave buses behind for a while. Once a week the ancient and splendid SS *Ollanta* meets the train at Puno and sets sail for the Bolivian port (on Lake Titicaca) of Guaqui, something over 100 miles away. The rules insist on this, even though the journey is far more frequently possible by bus, but even if it is necessary to wait six days for the boat it is worth doing since (by definition) time and money are no object and the steamer is an incredible 19th-century survival of great style and comfort, even if perhaps a little motheaten nowadays. Trains

Right:
A 3ft gauge Huancayo-Huancavelica Railway railcar at Huancayo station, Peru.

Extreme right:
The Peruvian Central Railway in steam days. A Beyer-Peacock 'Andes' type 2–8–0 locomotive heads the daily Lima-Huancayo train.

Passengers join the 3ft gauge
Huancayo-Huancavelica
Railway train at a wayside
halt in the high Peruvian
Andes.

Above:
A Peruvian steam-hauled train prepares to leave Macchu-Picchu station for Cuzco headed by 4–6–0 No 100.

Right:
Cochabamba station, Bolivia.

on the short railway from Guaqui to La Paz are now a bit erratic, since the railcars are rough and the mixed steam runs only occasionally. All the way from La Paz to Buenos Aires, 1500 miles of meter gauge, there is a twice-weekly passenger train. One is now really getting into civilized and populous parts. However, there is an alternative for those who have not yet seen sufficient Andean spectacle, and that is to detour from Oruro to Cochabamba by railcar, bus thence to Sucre, and back again in another railcar (or possible mixed steam) to the main line at Rio Mulato via Potosi, to see what the Bolivians can do with railway mountaineering – it does not suffer from comparison with anything seen before. Meanwhile, the main line runs across the high, arid, and rather dull altiplano plateau, actually reaching the highest points reached by rail in the world (until the Chinese get to Lhasa).

At Uyuni, still in Bolivia, one is faced with a situation unparalleled so far in this circumferroviacal tour of the South American continent; one has a choice between two all-rail routes. To reach the capital of Chile, Santiago, one can proceed either via Antofagasta and the Chilean northern longitudinal route down the western side of the Andes, or one can proceed into Argentina, via Tucuman, Cordoba and Mendoza on the original Transandine Railway. Each route is meter gauge throughout, except for the last few miles into Santiago on the Chilean main 5ft 6in gauge

system. Either way one will spend four or five days on the train, with recuperative overnight stops at Cordoba or Antofagasta; the practicalities of the choice of route are probably to be determined by the fact that there is but one train a week via Antofagasta, but at least twice as many on most of the Argentine route (Cordoba to Mendoza unfortunately runs only once a week, but Cordoba, as the pleasant city at the center of the sierras and vineyards of northern Argentina, is perhaps a better place to spend six days waiting for the next train than Antofagasta, the port serving the tin and guano industries). And scenically, a journey over the Transandine is more attractive than a trundle down the arid northern Chilean desert. Only the very rare and hardened traveller goes via Antofagasta; there are certainly bonus points of some sort to be earned that way.

South of Santiago, on the broad gauge, one is back (for a while) in the land of trains which run daily – indeed, of lines which carry more than one daily train. One should make the most of it. Southern Chile has one of the most beautiful landscapes on earth, and one of the most prosperous in South America. One leaves Santiago on electrified track; following an excellent dinner and comfortable night in a sleeping car, one wakes up beyond the end of the wires at San Rosendo to find oneself back in steam territory. Probably the passenger express will be diesel-hauled (but if the diesel breaks down, steam

The Bolivian Boat Train leaves Guaqui on Lake Titicaca for La Paz.

usually comes to the rescue), but certainly freights and branch-line trains will still be steam-worked, and by reasonably well-kept locomotives too, some of them modern. Branch lines diverge frequently towards the coast or up beautiful valleys leading towards lakes and volcanoes.

The end of the line is at Puerto Montt, some 700 miles south of Santiago; but much less than a day and a night is needed to cover this distance here, in contrast with the rate of progress till now. By this latitude the Andes, though still an impressive mountain range, have declined greatly and no longer present the same formidable obstacles that they once did. Consequently, the traveller has another choice for the next leg of his other journey, since he or she can travel either in one day from Puerto Montt to San Carlos de Bariloche in Argentina by bus or in two days by boat and bus using the chain of lakes which covers much of the distance. San Carlos de Bariloche is a winter sports and summer holiday center and is said to be Argentina's cleanest town, a distinction which means more in Argentina or Chile than it would have in some of the other countries already passed through. From here, another 5ft 6in gauge railway runs 1075 miles north and east to the capital, Buenos Aires, with a train which runs daily in summer and twice a week in winter.

As far as Bahia Blanca the going can be a bit rough and dusty; thereafter the fertility of the

country improves. One interesting detour on this section, south of Bahia Blanca, is a trip over the 2ft 6in gauge branch from Ingeniero Jacobacci to Esquel – 250 miles of very remote and rural, steam-worked and beautiful, if hardly economic, track. In Esquel and further south in Patagonia, it is still possible to hear Welsh spoken, though perhaps not quite the same Welsh that would pass in Wales today. Given time and cash one could penetrate much further south, in fact to another 2ft 6in gauge line and the southernmost railway in the world, the recently built and entirely steam-worked section from Rio Gallegos, 155 miles to the collieries at Rio Turbio, opened in 1951. Curiously enough, this outfit has never had anything to do with the Argentine Ministry of Railways since it was built and is operated by the Ministry responsible for collieries, and is chiefly notable for having the largest and most powerful, and very much the most advanced, steam locomotives ever to have run on any narrow-gauge railway anywhere (or for that matter on many standard or broad-gauge lines). Scenically, culturally and climatically, southern Patagonia can only be rated somewhere solidly below zero in any guide-book, but its steam power is one definite plus!

South America is a land of contrasts, and one of the most decided contrasts of all is the arrival in Buenos Aires along the four-track main line into the 15-platform Plaza Constitucion terminus

The weekly mixed train from Sucre to Potosi in Bolivia takes water at an isolated Andean watering point headed by Hitachi 2–8–2 No 671.

(one of many modern stations in the city). It is good to be reminded of the fact that the commuterland grind of Clapham Junction or Jamaica, Long Island, has its Latin American counterpart. Having rested among the comforts and delights of Buenos Aires, one can skip across the water (overnight steamer or hydrofoil both permissible) to Montevideo and relax again in the Uruguayan capital.

Uruguayan railways, like Argentine ones, are now recovering somewhat from a period of politically induced decrepitude, though neither have recovered sufficiently as yet to have banished all their remaining steam locomotives to the scrapyard. On the way north and east from Montevideo to Paysandu via the redolently-named focal point junction of Paso de los Toros, one is likely to see some of the survivors, though probably doing little more than shunting. More characteristic of this part of the world is the continuing sight of black-hatted and baggy-trousered gauchos rounding up their cattle. A short railcar journey on to Salto, and one crosses the wide Uruguay River to Concordia, back in Argentina (though in the standard-gauge province of it). The next train is (assuming one has calculated the day right) the twice-weekly one which carries through sleeping cars from Buenos Aires to Asuncion; the journey to the capital of Paraguay occupies two nights, beginning early on the first morning and arriving mid-afternoon on the third day.

Train ferries in northern Argentina are quite interesting ones. The ferry between Posadas and Encarnacion (Paraguay) is a particularly choice specimen, with a steam-powered haulage engine winding the coaches one by one off the boat and up the ramp, whence they are led up a switchback and along the streets of Encarnacion by a woodburning tank engine. The 231-mile main line of the President Carlos Antonio Lopez Rail-

Rolling stock of the privately owned Antofagasta and Bolivia Railway Company forms a train on the Northern Transandine Railway, Chile.

Left:
An Argentinian 3ft gauge double-headed train, northbound from Esquel to Ingeniero Jacobacci at El Maiten.

Below:
The Southern of Peru main line runs from Cuzco through Juliaca to the southern capital of Arequipa

Above:
Argentina: the British origins of Argentinian railways are clearly indicated by this view of a Vulcan Foundry 4–8–0 on a local train at Tandil. Note the semaphore signals.

Right:
A transandine train on the northern route, hauled by Henschel 2–10–2 No 1335. This photograph was taken from the bed of a Pullman sleeper.

way from Encarnacion to Asuncion takes our train 18 hours (with a little bit of luck), behind a fine old British-built woodburning 2–6–0 of 1910; eating in the lurching restaurant car is a little difficult because of the tendency of the crockery to fall out of the open window, and the tendency of passing wildlife (mainly insect) to come in by the same route. However, one eventually arrives at the immaculate marble platform of Asuncion's multi-columned station, to the sound of street-cars rattling past.

Actually, the trip to Paraguay is a detour; one could in fact have taken the other line from Paso de los Toros and crossed into Brazil, and then by meter gauge and various stages to São Paulo and Rio de Janeiro. In any case, although there is by no means any very cohesive long-distance system of passenger trains in southern Brazil, the route is possible about thrice-weekly, given a little dedication; and a very worthwhile detour in the area is, in any case, essential, to see the quite isolated but very fine Santa Catarina railway based at Tubarao. This is a coal-hauling line, the last important wholly-steam-worked line in Brazil, and impressive in the extreme with fine modern 2–10–4s hauling 1600-ton trains down to the sea at Imbituba. To reach it means a side-trip by bus, either from the Uruguay border to the São Paulo line, or equally possible all the way from Asuncion, in Paraguay, whence a road leads due eastwards to Brazil. There are several other railways in Paraguay, by the way, all running from ports and landing stages on the Paraguay River north and upstream from Asuncion; maps and directories show them, but no traveller known to the author has yet returned with any description of them and they must be regarded as subjects for the more advanced researcher.

São Paulo is Brazil's largest city, and a modern metropolis second to none. São Paulo also lies near one of the world's greatest railway oddities, the Serra Nova inclines, which carry the broad-gauge Santos-Jundiai Railway up the 3000ft escarpment of the Serra de Mar. Starting at Paranapiacaba, an hour by electric train from

Above:
No 3023 4–6–2 at Santa Fe,
Argentina.

Right:
A steam-worked
locomotive as used on the
famous rope-worked Serra
de Mar inclines of the
former Santos-Jundiai
Railway in Brazil.

the Luz station in São Paulo, the main part of the heavy freight and passenger traffic on this route is still taken up the steam-worked, rope-worked, 1 in 12 inclines, seven miles long, which date back to the opening of the railway at the turn of the century. Oil-fired steam 'streetcar-type' locomotives carry grips which fasten onto steel ropes, powered by immaculate steam stationary engines, and the combination of types of power passes traffic up five consecutive inclines, on each of which ascending and descending trains have to be balanced. The complexity of the operation is considerable, but it remains in full use alongside a newly-built electrified rack railway which simply takes part of the business. Both lines are cut into a steep mountainside, with a succession of tunnels and viaducts over deep ravines.

São Paulo to Rio de Janeiro, something over 300 miles, is perhaps the most important main line in Brazil; it is broad gauge and electrified. Unfortunately the passenger service on it is not very remarkable either for speed or frequency, though the equipment is good. Perhaps this is the moment to say that Brazilian railways have a policy of doing as little as possible to encourage passenger traffic – in fact they act positively to divert as much long-distance passenger business to road as possible. However, Rio is a beautiful and interesting enough city to attract attention, with much railway interest of its own. The yellow Carioca streetcars still teeter over their impressive double-arched viaduct (originally an aqueduct), high above the rooftops, on their way into the suburban hills of Santa Teresa, and the electrified rack Corcovado Railway still takes the passenger up to the amazing mountaintop statue of Christ. And for a final steam 'fix,' one can spend a couple of days on a slow excursion to the all-steam 2ft 6in gauge line from Antonia Carlos to São João del Rei, a couple of hundred miles northwest of the city. The daily passenger train to São João, an old colonial city with two beautiful 18th-century churches, is formed of a rake of

Woodburning North British Locomotive Company 2–6–0 No 58 heads a through Asuncion-Buenos Aires train.

brown wooden coaches hauled by a diminutive but spotless 1889-built American 2–8–0, antique perhaps but still able to run fast. The narrow gauge actually continues for a total of about 70 miles, and it is possible to return to Rio by another equally interesting route.

Rio de Janeiro would be a sensible place to end our South American tour, a high spot, and one of the most beautiful cities in the world. Any dedicated traveller who has come this far deserves to pass with honor into the small, select band of super-achievers in this very special field. The sad fact remains, however, that one has so far travelled around barely two-thirds of the continent. Thus, after a brief sojourn in Rio to recuperate, one must again take to the rails.

Meter gauge rails lead north again from Rio, either to Brasilia, the Monday to Friday ferro-concrete capital plonked down by politicians in the middle of the Amazonian jungle, or further along the coast and inland alternately and indirectly to Salvador, Recife, and ultimately São Luiz, round the corner and undeniably back on the north coast of the continent. But the next two thousand miles are disastrous; practically no

road for half the distance, and practically no railway either. Guyana, which once had the oldest railway in South America, now has nothing except an upstream, jungle-land, dieselized ore-hauler. Surinam may still have a steam train once a week, but no map of the area is of a large enough scale to show the two ends of its line as two separate points. Venezuela once had a marvellous narrow-gauge mountain line from La Guiara to Caracas, but blasted it to bits for a superhighway; they have large plans to build a new railway network somewhere else, and actually opened the first section of it, achieving within a matter of months a spectacular head-on collision. Thus, from the middle of Brazil back to our starting point, Santa Marta in Colombia, no rails exist now nor have ever existed, except locally in the Maracaibo oilfields. And so it's malarial jungles or back to Rio.

Needless to say, most visitors to South America will be forced to include airline tickets in their travel documents but any and all attempts at rail travel in this continent are rewards in themselves. No country is best seen from airports and this is particularly true of South America.

The meter-gauge Dona Teresa Christina Railway of Brazil. Here a Baldwin 2–10–2 with coal train nears Tubarao.

India and Pakistan

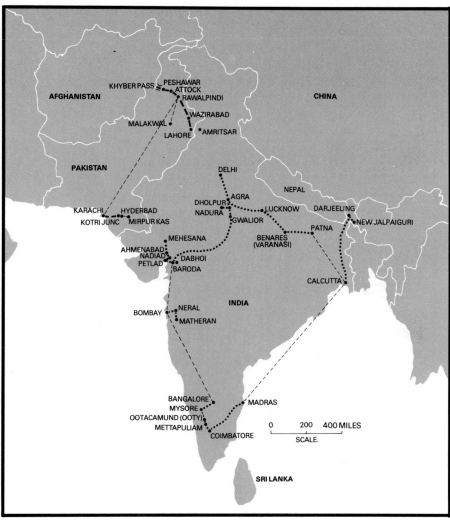

The 36,000-mile Indian rail system is by far the largest in the world to be generally open to any traveller who just simply buys a ticket. It is roughly 50 percent larger in route-mileage than the United States passenger network; in fact, the only system in the world larger than the Indian one is that of the USSR and a mere ticket does not constitute open access to the Soviet Railways. Furthermore India has by far the largest steam locomotive fleet in the world; it operates on both the narrowest of narrow and the broadest of broad gauges; and English is Indian Railways' mother tongue.

One must also consider before rushing off to enjoy India's railways that ten million passengers are carried by Indian Railways each day! Sometimes, waiting on an Indian station in company with a too large proportion of that ten million, one occasionally wishes that a passion for rail travel was a rarer thing in that country. It is significant that, for some routes and certain types of accommodation, one needs to book ahead six months and more. Similar remarks apply to Pakistan.

The writer, whose first visit to India was on his own, strongly suggests that others should not follow his example but, instead, do what he did on his second and third trips and go with a group.

An account follows, in the form of a cocktail mixture, telling of both the group tours. It contains, written between the lines, many 'dos and don'ts' in respect of Indian rail travel. The tours were arranged, respectively, by Bill Alborough, who runs tours under the name 'To Europe for Steam,' in 1975 and by Festiniog Travel in 1978. In both cases local arrangements in India were made by the Travel Corporation of India.

Nuts-and-bolts information on steam locomotives is not generally appropriate to this book, but an exception is made in the case of India, the 'steamiest' country in the world. Indian steam locomotive history can be divided into four overlapping periods. Primeval or non-standard (1852–1914), BESA (1903–1950), IRS (1926–1939) and post-war steam (1947–1972). During the Primeval period, 2–4–0s and 0–4–2s were the norm, although some lines had 4–6–0s long before such monsters were used in their home country. Broad-gauge non-standard steam locomotives have virtually disappeared, and they are very rare on the meter-gauge lines. The narrow gauge,

Bottom:
A gilded Jaguar and polished cup-type wind gauge are among the embellishments of this class WL 4–6–2 at Delhi Junction shed.

Below:
On Indian Railways' extensive 5ft 6in gauge network, two well-turned-out and rare class HSM 2–8–0s set off with a Khurda Junction to Puri train.

however, has many quaint survivors still doing excellent work.

The British Engineering Standards Association (BESA) designs were introduced in 1903, covering 4–6–0, 4–4–2 and 4–4–0 passenger designs and 2–8–0, 0–6–0 freight. The 4–6–0s were still being built as late as 1951. Corresponding 4–6–0s and other types were constructed for the meter gauge. Many BESA locomotives are still to be found working in 1978, a tribute to their sound design.

Alas, the same comment cannot be applied to the IRS designs, mainly consisting of 4–6–2s of three different sizes (XA, XB, XC), and two 2–8–2s (XD, XE). The Pacifics had a reputation of being poor steamers, sluggish runners and the XBs particularly, were bad riders to a point not of discomfort but of danger. In the end, at Bihta, in 1937, one derailed with the loss of 117 lives. An enquiry led to some modification, but the IRS broad-gauge designs never met the promises of their design committee, although some are still to be found in use. On the other hand the meter-gauge IRS YB 4–6–2s and YD 2–8–2s are satisfactory machines, while on the narrow gauge generally, the ZB 2–6–2s and ZE 2–8–2s remain the last word in steam power even today.

During World War II, Lend-Lease brought quantities of North American broad- and meter-gauge 2–8–2s to India. Their rugged characteristics showed up well in conditions there and led to an order being placed with Baldwins of the USA for the first batch of a new standard range of locomotives. So, in 1946, there arrived in India the first WP 4–6–2s. Further batches built in many countries brought the total to 755, later to be eclipsed by the WG 2–8–2s which reached 2450. There were also small WL 4–6–2s as well as three corresponding designs for the meter gauge, YP 4–6–2s, YG 2–8–2s and YL 2–6–2s. A handful of ZP narrow gauge 4–6–2s were also acquired, but insufficient for them to be regarded as a standard design. Some 40 percent of Indian steam is made up of these excellent post-war locomotives. Many were built in India, in particular at the Chittaranjan Locomotive Works, set up in 1950 with British aid in order to give India self-sufficiency in locomotive construction. Locomotive building was no new thing for India; contrary to popular belief, even in the days of the Raj several of the old companies built their own locomotives and coaches.

The once-weekly Pakistan Railways train on the Nushki Extension Railway threads uninhabited country en route for Persia. Only 150 miles separates the terminus of this line at Zahedan from rails which connect with those of Europe.

133

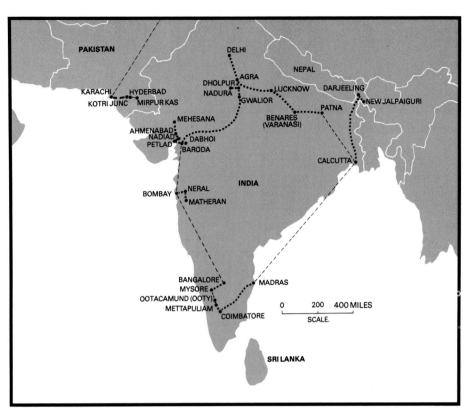

those live coelacanths of the locomotive world on the 2ft gauge at Neral, 0–6–0Ts with Sir Percival Heywood's design of flexible wheelbase system (side play on the center axle and *radial* movement on the outers). Sir Percival's creation did us proud on 45ft radius curves, which would normally be considered severe for $7\frac{1}{4}$in gauge and prohibitive on $10\frac{1}{4}$in. The first one had a big sign 'OOPS, WHAT A CURVE!' and our locomotive's way with a combination of this and a 1 in 20 grade would have done the old man's heart good. It must be noted that after *two* hours climbing Neral was still in sight far below.

Monkeys abounded in the woods round the little hill station of Matheran, where the group relaxed before departing on the booked diesel train back down the hill, steam having been specially arranged for our ascent. However, 'you

Route 14 'You Want Steam? I Put Steam On'

Most of us still do not really believe what we saw in this incredible land, possessor of a fleet of steam locomotives which is the world's largest by a factor of at least two. Was it only in a dream that we witnessed a decorated 2ft 6in gauge 2–6–2 being named *Mohindra* to honor a visiting Chief Mechanical Engineer with a charming ceremony that included flower-garlanding the leader and ladies of our party?

After an uneventful flight, the party's first sight of India was magnificently squalid urban Bombay, whose enterprising operators relieved members during the first few hours of both a wallet and a camera. Worse was to come, for awaiting the party leader was a letter announcing that photography of locomotive sheds would *not* be permitted. A certain blight was therefore cast over the first formal visit to Lower Parel Shed, where we saw two out of the three principal generations of 5ft 6in gauge Indian express power (post-war WP 4–6–2 and BESA 4–6–0) specially cleaned and paraded for our benefit in perfect conditions, while cameras languished under guard in the locomotive foreman's bungalow. The day was not completely lost, however, for our Travel Corporation of India coach went on to give us some excellent lineside steam picture opportunities on the Western Railway main line. TCI made all the arrangements in India, the main burden falling on their couriers who accompanied the party throughout.

The tour started with 'Matheran Monday', an outing on the Central Railway, beginning at Bombay Victoria Terminus. Indian Railways' origins are absolutely clear when one finds that the Western Railway terminus is called Central! What a pleasure to see early-electric English 'crocodile' locomotives in action on the CR main line to Poona, but it is nothing to that of finding

want steam, I put steam on' was the station-master's reply to someone's diffident enquiry and so it was. Good news awaited our return, in that having carried the matter as far as Delhi, it had been established that the ban on photography would not apply to steam locomotives but only to their installations.

Tuesday morning was devoted to a rarely granted privilege, a visit to the Bombay Port Trust's elegant steam power (Vulcan/Nasmith-Wilson 2–6–0Ts in use plus stored 2–10–2Ts), followed by a rather more productive visit to Lower Parel Shed, a rapid but excellent lunch at Hotel Transit near the airport and lastly an Indian Airlines flight north to Ahmenabad, the capital of Gujerat State.

'I wonder what they feed it on' said someone as we contemplated the disreputable local bus

laid on to take the party to the pleasantly oriental Cama Hotel for the usual brief night before 'Meter Gauge' Wednesday. However, the orientality of the hotel did not prevent it from serving porridge with its pre-dawn breakfast and, after a few mouthfuls, instantly it became broad daylight. Sabermarti Junction Shed was the first call and, for most, it was also the first sight of the huge meter-gauge network, 16,000 miles in extent – on its own 50 percent larger than British Rail – which rivals the broad gauge in size but which is really very little known. We met the very fine scaled-down versions of Indian standard broad gauge locomotives (YP 4–6–2, YG 2–8–2, YL 2–6–2) plus a good collection of interesting older types, including some 4–6–0s, 4–6–4Ts, and, my wife was delighted to note, some YB 4–6–2s, products of her home town of Darlington.

An Indian 2ft gauge 0–6–0T locomotive hauls a train from Neral. These locomotives can negotiate 45ft radius curves.

The gateway to Indian Railways – Victoria Terminus, Bombay.

The next event was a 60-mile meter-gauge ride north to Mehesana behind a YP 4–6–2 in two special first-class reserved bogies marshalled at the front. Double track stretched across the plains of India, the wide spacing proportionate to the gauge reminding one of the Romney, Hythe & Dymchurch Railway in Kent, England, just as the YP did in following Henry Greenly's narrow-gauge proportions. It was wonderful to look out and see traditional British-style lower-quadrant semaphores – distant, home, starter pulled off at a nice angle for us at each station – and occasionally pass other steam coming the other way. Mehesana and another big locomotive shed, into which we were taken complete with our bogies, came all too soon. Finally, after superb loco-motive viewing and train watching there, we were *attached* to an immense 20-coach diesel-hauled '1 Down' 'Delhi Mail' to return to Ahmenabad, perhaps just a trifle jaded after a very long and rather hot day. No bus appeared to take us back to the hotel, but instead, a fleet of two-seat motorized three-wheel rickshaws; spirits rose as we raced through the packed city streets to dinner and the odd hour or so in bed.

More pre-dawn porridge and we were off by electric train to Nadiad where the shed had all

the charm of narrow-gauge independence, for these 2ft 6in gauge railways were, until a few years ago, the personal property of a very great rail fan, HRH the Gaekwar of Baroda. A Yugoslavian-built standard ZB 2–6–2 and an old Bagnall 0–6–4T were swung on the table in the sunshine for us, while we in our turn provided entertainment for the local population, as well as their animals. At all the sheds we went to, the viewing of locomotives was followed by kind hospitality in the form of welcome cups of tea, together with particularly interesting conversations on the best of all subjects. Nadiad was specially nice as we sat in the shade of a creeper-covered loggia watching Indian squirrels frisking around in the foliage.

Soon it was train time and the Bagnall was nosing across a lozenge (rather than a diamond) crossing over the broad gauge with a big packed train and we became part of the countryside in the way road transport never does. One rubbed one's eyes to see wild peacocks wandering in the fields and then, wonder of wonders, a run-past . . . and on a service train, too. The only problem was that lots of the other passengers descended and ran past with the train too. After a meet with a ZB (nice Old English semaphores again), Petlad came all too soon. A WL light standard 4–6–2 took us on the broad gauge to Anand for a shed visit and lunch in the first-class ladies and gents waiting rooms, made co-ed for this occasion. Incidentally, a sidelight on Indian social conditions is that first-class fares are approximately six times the second class, the latter being modestly set at around $2 (£1) for 200 miles.

We travelled electric to Baroda, with a stop short of the station for the party to descend,

cross running lines and a hump yard with humping in progress, to visit the shed. Nicely polished standard types, plus a superb and quintessentially British BESA 4–6–0, gleamed in the now ideally angled sunshine; then we transferred, once again by rickshaw at a high speed, to our Hotel Utsara to get, for once, a nice early night in preparation for one of the red-letter days of the tour, 'Dabhoi' Day. The Chief Mechanical Engineer of the Western Railway, Mr Mohindra Singh, honored us by deciding to take the opportunity of making a visit to Dabhoi on the day we were due there. Dabhoi is a meeting point of five 2ft 6in gauge branches, all once part of the princely Baroda system and has forests of traditional lower quadrant semaphores and British-type fully gated level crossings. These really came into their own as a hurly-burly of ox and camel carts, livestock and people, whose appearance could hardly have changed since Biblical times, poured across. It also has a shed with an allocation of over 30 ZBs, plus 4–6–0s and 2–8–4Ts.

However, when the great man arrived, everything went well and after a dignified forehead daubing and garlanding ceremony, a curtain was pulled back to reveal a ZB whose dazzling décor made the eyes blink. Fretted brass plates shone in the sunshine and such touches as a duck or dove silhouetted on the chimney and a revolving wind-gauge on the dome told of a dedication to and a love of steam which made us take Dabhoi Shed and its staff to our hearts: and they named the engine *Mohindra* to honor their chief.

One might think anything else would be an anti-climax, but not so, for miniature fans anyway, because in the afternoon we came upon a real lost treasure, the ex-Surrey Border and

India's meter-gauge system: standard class YP 4–6–2s 2448 and 2499 cross at Kaparpura.

Camberley Railway miniature 10¼in gauge LNER Pacific built by tragic Charles Bullock in 1938 for that ambitious but only briefly existing line. She was hard at work in the municipal park (previously the Palace grounds), having been lost without trace for some 35 years. Footplate riding (yes, literally) was also indulged in nearby on some elephantine 0–1–1–1–1–0s with an extremely heavy axle-load rating.

On the following day, a few members and ex-members of British Rail staff with the group (including the writer) were treated to a tour of the Indian Railway Staff College, previously the Royal Heir's Palace. 'We have re-organized today's program so you can give us a talk,' said the Principal over coffee amidst the painted animals on the walls of what had once been the Royal Nursery. However, all must be forgiven, for we were then shown what must be one of the most wonderful model railways in existence. There were 23 working signal boxes, fully interlocked with proper block or tablet instruments, set out in a great hall with track (about 2in gauge) and complete signalling, representing all the kinds of railway working to be found on Indian Railways. A trick was missed, I think, for those of the party to indulge in the no doubt

humbling experience – for self-styled railway experts – of working the layout.

The party then regrouped to travel overnight to Delhi. Long distance travel by rail in India is what might be called an acquired taste and few had a comfortable night. In mitigation, although the train was diesel hauled, steam was visible in the moonlight almost whenever one looked out. But, on arrival at Delhi, real beds in the Hotel Akbar never seemed more inviting. Duty, however, drove us out sightseeing; most memorable of the sights were the Lutyens' Government Buildings in New Delhi. The next day, also in New Delhi, there was an opportunity to see the superb railway museum, created by another Englishman, Michael Satow, who is currently engaged in organizing the Inter-City 150 jamboree in Britain. The 2–2–2 *Fairy Queen* of 1870 to the Bengal-Nagpur 4–8–0+0–8–4 Garratt of 1935 delineates the range of a collection which magnificently represents Indian railway development, apart, that is, from some notable absentees which will be available when they finally go out of use in a few years.

At Delhi shed, the staff had vied with Dabhoi in decorating an old inside cylinder BESA 0–6–0 and a modern WL light 4–6–2. The latter included

India's narrow-gauge system: a standard class ZB 2ft 6in gauge 2–6–2 at Nadiad.

in its décor a golden Jaguar in front of the smokebox.

The next morning at 0645 hours and in spite of being under the bows of the flagship, the driver of the 43 down 'Taj Express' saw no reason why members of the party should not ride with him on his 4–6–2 and in this way Agra was reached by mid-morning. May one say that the beauty of the Taj Mahal is such that it took away any thoughts of steam and all voted to return that evening to see it again in the moonlight. Add the fact that Clark's Shiraz Hotel had a resident elephant available for rides and one can imagine that railways for one short half-day at least took a back seat.

The next day was 'Dholpur' day. If Dabhoi in far off Baroda represents large scale narrow gauge, Dholpur, south of Agra, is the headquarters of a pocket-size 2ft 6in system. It has a wonderful Boston Lodge style works (Boston Lodge is the repair shop of that grand-daddy of all narrow gauge, the Festiniog Railway) in which ageing 2–8–4Ts from Hunslet of England and 4–8–0s from Hanomag of Germany are put into order, while rolling stock is built from scratch. The group's accommodation on the 10.45 train included the old Maharajah's saloon and the group's depleted numbers, after allowing for those AWOL on their way to the delights of

the 2ft gauge in Gwalior, 40 miles to the south, could just be accommodated. The bus which had brought us to Dholpur met the train at Napura station down the line.

The special first-class bogie attached that evening for us to the 'Avadh Express' for Lucknow (steam, electric and diesel traction in succession) had had less than a first-class cleaning; although, to compensate, the rolls of bedding (complete with towel and inflatable pillow) in their canvas covers were brand-new. Lucknow had temples, broad and meter-gauge sheds (including BESA 4–6–0s and a rare IRS WM 2–6–4T) and, of course, a Residency, still lovingly cared for under Indian Independence more than 120 years after the famous siege was lifted.

Lucknow to Varanasi was a daytime ride; marshalled next to the group's special bogie was an Indian Railways second-class Tourist Car, in which a party (organized by Butterfield's Tours of Leeds, England) was living while rolling by rail round India. Accommodation was primitive with wooden do-it-yourself bunks and a cast-iron coalburning range, on which a cauldron of homemade marmalade was simmering away.

Sunrise over the Ganges, with the group out on the waters in a cockle-shell row-boat, was everything it had been said to be, but the visit to Benares was overshadowed by an uncertainty in

A 2ft 6in gauge train from Rajim to Raipur crosses a typically Indian bridge. Class CC 4–6–2 No 664 heads the train.

Above:
Dabhoi Locomotive Depot, India. A superbly decorated class ZB 2–6–2 No 89 is officially named *Mohindra* in honor of the local Chief Mechanical Engineer.

Superbly polished and embellished locomotives at Delhi Junction Shed, India. From left to right they are a class SGC 0–6–0, a class WL light 4–6–2 and a class WP 4–6–2.

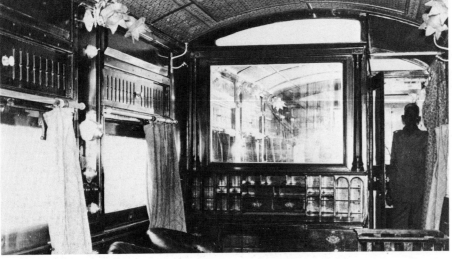

Above:
Interior of the Maharajah's saloon on India's Dholpur line.

Top:
India's Dholpur line. Seen here is a 2ft 6in gauge Hunslet 2–8–4T.

respect of the onward flight (by Indian Airlines) to Calcutta, on which so much depended. In the end, some had the bonus of an extra five-hour train trip to Patna, with the sight of a BESA 2–8–0 in the station.

Howrah Shed at Calcutta was an enclave of order in one of the world's most overcrowded and poverty-ridden cities. Among the treasures on display was the first IRS steam locomotive seen, an XC 4–6–2, described by some as that 'great Henry Greenly Pacific.'

It was now time to begin the great Darjeeling adventure. At Sealdah terminus the intrepid travellers formed a 'British Square' among the first Indian crowd we met whose intentions and mood were not obviously friendly. Meanwhile, the TCI courier and his helpers performed the remarkable feat of getting our luggage out of the buses and on to the train amongst this predatory melée of poverty-stricken humanity. Each suitcase on the trolley had a rope passed through each individual handle. However, all was well and soon enough we were settled in first-class compartments on one of the world's very few named steam expresses, the 'Darjeeling Mail.' (Alas, since this was written it has become diesel-hauled.)

A few were offered footplate rides which could only be described as a total experience; 100 kilometers per hour on this Pacific made 100mph on a British Gresley (noted for its good riding) very tame. Anyway, imagine a rocking, roaring locomotive, tearing at what seemed to be about twice the speed of sound through the moonlit night, tended by a crew of four undoubtedly enjoying themselves in a huge cab which had ample room for the six of us. It was also notable for an equally huge and disconcerting gap between cab and tender side-sheets. The writer was particularly impressed with a display of the legendary English *sang-froid* on the part of his companion, as the white-hot end of a firebox pricker was passed within six inches of his ear as we lurched over some particularly rough points and crossings. Very few were awake for the impressively long crossing of the Ganges over the great barrage at Farakka, for the group had by now acquired the trick of sleeping in an Indian sleeper! Like old campaigners, we now knew how to set to and make some pretty basic facilities into reasonable comfort, even having showers in the washrooms.

Approaching New Jalpaiguri (change for the Himalayas, now coming into view) there was an excellent view of the parallel meter-gauge Assam main line – with some action – in the excellent morning light, a bonus which was compensation for a 1½-hour late arrival. In spite of there being minus-30 minutes to make the Darjeeling connection, it appeared that there was quite a program for us. This consisted of an excellent breakfast as well as a pilgrimage to the 2ft gauge running shed. Here, tantalizingly under a photographic ban (New Jalpaiguri is close to the Bangladesh border and no one could get us dispensation there) were the rare and beautiful – but now out of use – Darjeeling Pacifics, once used on the 'plains' section of the line.

The Engineer of the Darjeeling-Himalayan section, Mr Cyrill, and several of his assistants met and conducted us personally. We had our own special fourth portion of 'The Mail' consisting of four named first-class cars – including the famous observation car *Everest* – and a van. All this took time and the three regular portions had long since vanished, coupled together for the 'plains' run to Sukna, when we were ready to depart. It had been intended to offer us the oldest of the famous 0–4–0Ts, No 777 (Sharp Stewart,

1889), but a mechanical defect meant we had 803 (North-British, 1928), one of the newest of the 24 which currently exist.

A pause at Siliguri produced some of the best meter-gauge shots of the tour with brown YP 4–6–2s and black WD 2–8–2 'McArthurs' of the North-East Frontier Railway. An uneventful toddle then brought the party to Sukna among the tea bushes. Perhaps some of the party were wondering what all the fuss over the DHR was about. . . .

They did not wonder for long as 803 left Sukna 'wide open' and we hit the 1 in 20 with frequent curvature of less than 1 chain radius that, in the

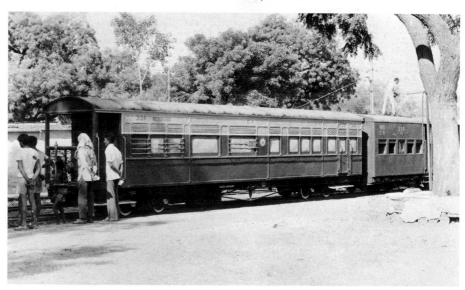

Bottom:
A Hanomag 4–8–0 at Napura station, on India's Dholpur line.

Below:
Former Maharajah's saloon on India's Dholpur line.

course of the next eight hours would take us clear of 7000ft altitude and in sight of mountains up to 29,000ft. At each Z-reverse the party spread themselves over the mountain sides (at least those did who were not with the brakesmen on the coach roofs) and at 'Agony Point' loop we had an official run-past. Tindaria works was, alas, out of bounds (too near the Chinese frontier this time!) but at Gaybari nearby we crossed the three portions of the 'Down Mail' with much flagging and general railway operating fun. By Kurseong where we stopped for tea, the light had gone – the penalty of our late start – and the remainder of the journey was in darkness mitigated by candles bought in the bazaar of one of the villages along whose main (and only) street we ran. Water stops passed pleasantly as we entertained (?) the villagers to candle-lit carols, and in between enjoyed the near perfect exhaust music of little 803.

The next day was also interesting and began with a 4 am call to attempt (unsuccessfully) to see sunrise on Everest from Tiger Hill. A fleet of taxis then began a vertical and horizontal train chase that can seldom have been equalled. The quality of the scenes meant that several people were well into their second hundred slide exposures on this one day alone. There was one man who scored 125 in spite of having succumbed (that day) to the intestinal ailment which plagued most of the group. Another was so excited by the most wonderful railway in the world that he exposed his standard 8 movie film twice! Such are the hazards of train-spotting on the Darjeeling line.

Other pleasures of Darjeeling included an evening watching Nepalese dancing and drinking millet beer in the magnificent ballroom of the Everest Hotel, while water cascaded through the roof and down the chandeliers. Millet beer is brewed in the tankard, the tankard being a section of bamboo stem – the brew is drunk through a straw and is surprisingly good. It was sad to leave the Himalayas, by taxi to Bagdogra Airport and plane to Madras.

In most of India the pressure of the huge popula-

Above:
India's broad gauge system. Standard class WG 2–8–2s at Bagwanpur.

Left:
A Darjeeling-Himalayan line train negotiates the bazaar at Kurseong.

147

tion with its resulting poverty and squalor – all of which tends to be exposed rather nakedly in the railway stations – is, to say the least, a little disconcerting to the visitor. The south in general and Madras in particular, is just that much better off; in fact, the human condition in Madras station is no worse and no better than that in London's Waterloo or New York's Grand Central. The same applies to the trains; no one has to sit on the buffers or on the roof of the 'Nilgiri Hills Express,' while our reserved bogie was clean and inviting, with all the fans and lights working. The WP

4–6–2 on the point was also clean and well maintained. To the writer, who spent many years caring for British permanent way, it was a real pleasure to look out as the headlight of the great locomotive bored its way through the Indian night, and admire the superbly maintained track. The way she rode at speed indicated that this was no illusion.

Full delicious English breakfast came aboard at Coimbatore; cornflakes, fried eggs, toast, jam and coffee, plus the news that the meter-gauge rack railway, which had been closed for several weeks

A Darjeeling-Himalayan line train enters the switchback above Tindaria (note the hand signal being given to driver).

because of a landslide, had re-opened for freight trains that very day. One was spotted as our minibuses climbed the serpentine hill road and several of the Swiss-built rack locomotives were in steam at system headquarters, Coonor, situated half-way up. Rides on the end galleries of the freight cars were offered, a little disconcerting when crossing bridges without guard rails or parapets.

The Savoy Hotel at Ootacamund with its excellent cuisine and its bungalow-bedrooms was almost the final treat. Some took rides on rather narrow-gauge horses and others were rewarded for early rising by the sight of a very charming baby elephant (he could only just walk) in a game park on the drive down.

A final stop at Bangalore produced not only a rare IRS XD 2–8–2 and an even rarer narrow gauge post-war ZP 4–6–2, but also much meter-gauge standard steam power in superbly groomed condition. Then it only remained to take the Airbus to Bombay, consume a superb dinner in the excellent Hotel Centaur, and thus return home by jumbojet.

Outside, we waited for the transit drivers to end their prayers and then made for Sainjees Motel. Pakistan has only just started to get to grips with tourism and the hotels were rather more basic than in India; peeling bedroom walls and utilitarian bathrooms were the norm.

Some of the party wanted another look at the station, but there was some difficulty in finding a conveyance. Eventually 13 large Englishmen piled into the smallest of Honda pick-ups, returning by horse and trap to find our rooms being sprayed with insect repellant, a nice touch as wasps of 747 proportions had been seen. The

Route 15 'Chicken Bones Are "On" Sir'

The visit to Pakistan started at Karachi (reached by air) and began with an eight-hour train ride to Hyderabad. The route was completely diesel as far as Kotri Junction, on the banks of the Indus opposite Hyderabad, so necks were craning out of unbarred windows as we drew in, looking for smoke. Three oil-fired British-built BESA 2–8–0s were busy on the shunt, the clean and exceptionally well-maintained appearance of the 1920 locomotives making a pleasing sight – so cameras into action! As we left we had our first sight of a virtually pure 'Derby' locomotive, a BESA 0–6–0.

dinner of soup, chicken curry and rice was to become familiar.

Breakfast call was at 04.30 am – for an 05.15 bus; the plan next morning was to visit Pakistan's only meter-gauge line, based on Mirpur Khas, by the o600 train; in this way we could use the early morning light. The broad-gauge pilot at Mirpur Khas was a BESA 2–8–o, while the meter gauge was very busy with 4–6–os and others readying trains in superb sunlight. The visit to the shed revealed some real gems among the oil-strewn ballast; old 4–6–os of various classes and BESA HG 2–8–os were there in profusion.

Tuesday began with a road trip to Karachi and a flight to Rawalpindi; we stayed at Gatmell's Motel with its chalet rooms. The writer reached his just in time to prevent moths from completely finishing off the pillow, but a roaring gas fire made a nice and cosy welcome.

Operation Malakwal was launched at 04.30 when alarm bells rang to start the five-hour trip in search of Pakistan's best steam center. I say 'five hours,' because this was the guide's estimate, but two road closures kept us on the road for six and one-half hours – a real treasure hunt it was at times with our small-scale maps. The last two hours took us over amazingly narrow rural roads choked with transport hauling in the sugar harvest. By the end of this epic thrash we were all saddlesore, but there was definitely gold at the end of the rainbow, because on shed we're seven BESA 4–4–os, nine IRS XA 4–6–2s, as well as twelve BESA 0–6–os. Working 4–4–os are now almost unknown elsewhere in the world.

We were all kept very busy over the next two-and-a-half hours photographing six steam-hauled passenger trains, and the sight and sound of working 4–4–os rocketed our spirits. Hordes of local children tended to make nuisances of themselves by running around and getting in the way of cameras. At 15.20 the long return trip began back to our chicken curry dinner.

The next day enabled us to re-charge our batteries travelling by train to Peshawar, accommodated in a special observation saloon attached to the rear of the train for our exclusive use. The journey took us through pleasing under-populated country with the distant frontier mountains getting nearer. A fine view of the grand British-built fort as we crossed the wide river gorge at Attock melded with more 0–6–os, while a journey by horse and trap at dusk to the Park Hotel completed the day, except of course for a chicken curry and rice dinner.

Three class SPS 4–4–os and one class SGS 0–6–o 'on shed' at Malakwal Locomotive Depot, Pakistan.

Couplings to the Khyber! Immaculate BESA 0–6–0s No 2530 and No 2502 headed and tailed three coaches and two wagons – with our observation saloon in the rake – for the Fridays Only 0900 to Landi Kotal. Our first stop was at an Air Force Base to allow a plane to land! The airfield's main runway crossed the Khyber line, but unfortunately photography of this exciting phenomenon was strictly forbidden. The first scheduled stop was at Jamrud, where members of the Khyber Rifles embarked complete with their Lee-Enfield rifles, to form the armed escort for the train through the wild tribal lands where even today the only law is local law. The line began its steady climb and the truly exciting part of the journey began. Riding point on the buffer beam of the leading locomotive, two men kept a keen eye on the track ahead, ensuring none had been removed by enterprising bandits!

The locomotives thrashed up barren mountain grades, through tunnels and into the first reversal station at Medenak. Then, with much oily clag, we blasted away in the opposite direction to the next reversal station – Changai – to be greeted by several members of our own party! Changai is directly above Medenak and a kindly railwayman had shown them the goat track up through the rocks. The terrain was now both rugged and wild, meeting all expectations, and eventually we reached Shahgai for a 30-minute water stop.

The leading locomotive stood next to a water crane while the rear locomotive trundled back down the track to another crane at the loop end. Local vendors came out of the rocks, live chickens being the main items for sale.

Refreshed, the locomotives resumed the hammer for 40 minutes to Landi Kotal, a quiet and desolate spot, with a detachment of Khyber Rifles waiting to unload their supplies from the wagons before they fell into local hands. The extensive sidings were locked out of use, only the passenger and freight platforms being in regular use. For us, there were the delights of the frontier town, a confusion of mud, trucks, buses, mule trains and so on. The world's most unhygenic butchers shop was matched by the state of the

A class SGS 0–6–0 powers the Fridays-only train from Landi Kotal to Peshawar Cantonment, on the Khyber Pass Line, Pakistan.

local dogs and mules – not a place to visit after dark, we felt.

All too soon, it was time to return; running downhill, our locomotives had little to do save apply the brakes occasionally. A photo run-past was done across a very nice bridge, oily smoke providing a striking picture. To complete a great day a *mutton* dinner was enjoyed at the Hotel. Soup was 'extra' at the Romantic Overlander's price of 75 pence ($1.50) per bowl.

Saturday saw us traversing the land by train again, and confusion at the station over seat reservations made for some lively debate, but was soon resolved and we settled down in a long line of window seats. The 'Awam Express' for Lahore left on time but, with pathing difficulties on the long single line sections, was far from express. Even so, on-train catering was provided and at the appointed hour, a group of us fought our way over heaps of bodies and baggage to the diner. To eat on trains is always fun, but once again it was chicken curry with rice. To keep things humming along, a cripple and two beggars

started working the train, the first such unfortunates we had seen for a few days. We were also introduced to the delight of freshly cut sugar cane freely distributed by a local merchant in our bogie. Eventually city lights denoted Lahore had been reached at last – from before sunrise to after sunset on the same train with the same locomotive.

The next day at Lahore was spent visiting the locomotive workshops (in the morning) and the Changa Manga Forest railway after lunch. This 2ft gauge system provides steam rides for tourists, using 0–6–0s from John Fowler of Bombay. Some posh BESA 0–6–0s were also seen; these work the 'International Trains' to India. They are decked out in stylish livery incorporating white wheels, red running plates, brass numerals and full lining out.

On the last day it was decided to end on a high note by going to see another group of those 4–4–0s (from Wazirabad) in action from the lineside. A high note it certainly turned out to be; five were seen, all spotless and in beautiful sunshine. So ended a wonderful trip.

Bottom:
Class SPS 4–4–0 No 2970 at Wazirabad, Pakistan.

Below:
The Fridays-only train on the Khyber Pass line, with SGS 0–6–0s front and rear, awaits departure from Landi Kotal station, Pakistan close to the Afghanistan border.

Southern Africa

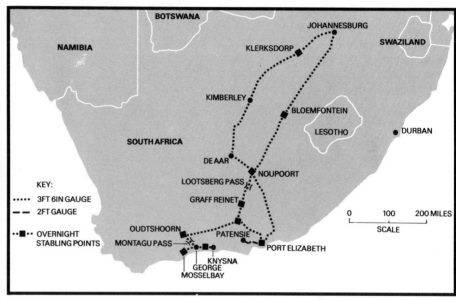

KEY:

····· 3FT 6IN GAUGE

--- 2FT GAUGE

■ OVERNIGHT STABLING POINTS

BOTSWANA

NAMIBIA

SWAZILAND

JOHANNESBURG

KLERKSDORP

KIMBERLEY

BLOEMFONTEIN

SOUTH AFRICA

LESOTHO

DURBAN

DE AAR

NOUPOORT

LOOTSBERG PASS

GRAFF REINET

OUDTSHOORN

PATENSIE

MONTAGU PASS

PORT ELIZABETH

KNYSNA

GEORGE

MOSSELBAY

0   100   200 MILES

SCALE

In general terms, southern African trains are receding in their attraction to the traveller. The furthest place north which a traveller by rail from the southernmost point of the continent could in theory reach without taking to the road at all is in Uganda, at present not a country to be recommended to inquisitive visitors. Kenya, of course, is excellent and still runs some steam trains although only for a few more years. Angola (which has the wonderful Benguela Railway, mostly powered by locomotives fired on eucalyptus wood) is out of reach after the recent Communist take-over and so also is Mozambique. Zaire and Zimbabwe are also unknowns.

This leaves South Africa itself and South African Railways, while still an efficient and incredibly impressive organization, make it very clear in various ways that they would prefer you to use their airline, South African Airways. Two exceptions are noted; first the de-luxe 'Blue Train' (from Johannesburg to Cape Town) and then its lesser known cousin, the 'Drakensberg Express,' from Johannesburg to Durban. These are two of the very few regularly scheduled trains in the world that are truly de-luxe, as defined in the introduction.

The use of superb steam locomotives has of course been a tremendous draw; even now the use of them on long-distance express trains has not quite come to an end. Some have taken their enthusiasm to extreme lengths; for example, in recent years, young and dedicated British enthusiasts have gone to South Africa to take jobs as firemen on the railways. This has been possible because all footplate work is in the 'white' sector, and native white South Africans are not too keen on the manual labor and the dirt involved in firing locomotives.

The timetable indicates that SAR provides three classes, but *apartheid* doubles this. The 'white' classes are first de-luxe (only on 'Blue Train' and 'Drakensberg'), first ordinary and second. Then there are 'black' first (only on a few trains), second and third, these latter being usually marshalled at the head of the train. It is not so much that the grime and smuts are worse near the locomotive (though that no doubt was also a consideration), but stations are arranged with 'white' and 'black' concourses, entrances, footbridges, subways and exits, so designed that carriages reserved for each ethnic group come to a conveniently positioned stand.

Speeds on the 3ft 6in gauge are not fast; for example, the 'Blue Train' only averages 36mph for its 1001-mile run. The train from Cape Town to Port Elizabeth over the wonderful Garden Route only manages an overall speed of 16mph for a 680-mile ride between places only 400 miles apart as the crow flies. Not slow enough, many who have made the trip will say! But alas, dieselization has just taken place on this line.

On the lines which are not electrified, therefore, SAR finds itself at the present time in limbo between being a steam railway and being a diesel one. While steam lasts, this and other circumstances gives them the opportunity to offer lovers of railways something very special as regards perfection in train travel.

South Africa's 'Blue Train' ascends the Hex River Pass, hauled by three matching electric locomotives.

In the introduction the qualities that define a *train de-luxe* were set out; in Chapter V a journey in such a train as near the ultimate imaginable as regards comfort and luxury was described by Mr Carew (the one at the Manchurian and Korean end of the trans-Siberian railway). But if one reads it carefully he will see that perfection still eludes him, even apart from the fact that the train concerned has not run for 60 years; for example, the scenery was bleak and poverty-stricken and in any case most of it went by at night. Also, it may be very nice to have a train to oneself occasionally, but most people prefer company.

The 'Sunset Limited,' sponsored by the Railway Society of Southern Africa, and organized by SAR, is an attempt to reach out just that one little bit further towards perfection in rail travel. First, accommodation is wholly in first-class sleeping, lounge and dining cars and that gives de-luxe status. Then, each night the train is stabled for the night and becomes a hotel, but without the trauma of transfers, registration, unpacking and packing. And should anyone oversleep, the train does not leave him behind.

An evening departure on Day 1 from Johannesburg's great station (the third on the present site) brings the traveller to the first item on the menu – something that is almost a contradiction in terms – to wit, a South African high-speed locomotive. SAR had a momentary brainstorm around 1934 and ordered six big-wheeled (6ft 0in diameter) Pacifics from Henschel of Germany for their 3ft 6in gauge tracks. These would comfortably be capable of over 70mph but, having bought these racehorses, SAR continued to run cart-horse-speed trains. Soon enough, the onset of World War II led to the idea being shelved while extended electrification and putting impatient travellers into the air removed the motivation. Anyway, one class 16E 4–6–2 out of the six survives as a curiosity and for occasions like this.

Most of the locomotives provided were, however, from normal service on the system and ranged in age from the class 12A 4–8–2 built by the North British Locomotive Company of Glasgow, Scotland, in 1912, to those class GMA Beyer-Garratts which came from Beyer-Peacock

Route 16
Steam Hotel

Bottom:
A South African 'Steam Safari' cruise train – a class 24 2–8–4T leading, class GMA Beyer-Garratt 4–8–2 +2–8–4 behind. Note separate water tank car for the GMA.

Below:
Unrivalled luxury – the dining car of the famous South African 'Blue Train.'

of Manchester in 1958, one of that great firm's (and Britain's) last sizeable orders for steam power; a feast for the ferro-equinologist, as well as being the ultimate for those who appreciate railways as an art form.

After Klerksdorp, overnight stabling points were, in order, Noupoort, Port Elizabeth (two nights), Klipplaat, Wilderness (near Knysna), Mossel Bay (Santos Beach), Oudtshoorn, Graaf Reinet, and Springfontein. Johannesburg was regained on the evening of the eleventh day. Santos Beach was particularly nice; one could, and did, descend from one's sleeper onto the beach and plunge straight into the Indian Ocean.

Other high spots were, (i) a triple-header with class 24 2–8–4s on the branch from George to Knysna and back; (ii) a fabulous day out on the 2ft gauge 'Apple Express' from Port Elizabeth to Loerie, Patensie, and back; (iii) the exuberance of two 60-year-old 4–8–2s, out on the main line from George to Mossel Bay after years of shunting in the Capetown yards; (iv) crossing the wild Lootsberg Pass with two engines up front, one to rear. In every case, the steam power was polished like jewelry.

And what of the train? The uniform line of clerestory roofs was very elegant, and the wood-panelled cabins comfortable. Of the meals, one can only say the trip was a gastronomic treat of the first order. All praise to the dining car staff, who produced nearly 4000 of these excellent meals in the ten days.

The fact that the trip was a sell-out leads one to anticipate similar ones being regularly offered to the public over the next few years. But not, alas, beyond that time, for even South African steam is not immortal.

Left:
A class 15 CA 4–8–2, built by the American Locomotive Company, heads a passenger train near Empangeni, South Africa.

Below:
The penalty of steam operation – the fireman of the 'Sunset Limited' cleans the fire.

Australasia

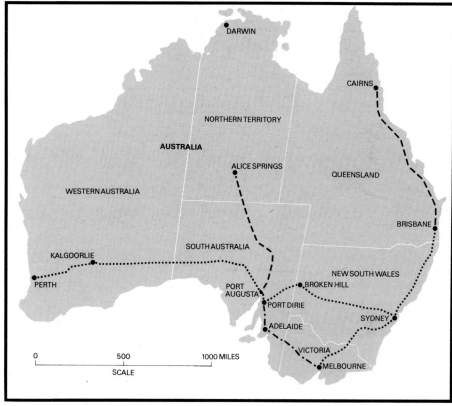

One must climb out of the rut and avoid journalistic clichés; it is therefore important, when commencing to write about Australian railroads, to kick off with some comment that is *not* about the notorious confusion of gauges in that continent. For this reason there will be no mention of the fact that, although the two main and several minor 3ft 6in gauge systems comprise 43 percent of the national network, by route mileage, they have always been in every other respect a scorned and derided minority, held greatly inferior in all ways to the 4ft 8½in lines of New South Wales (and extensions) or even the 5ft 3in wide undertakings in Victoria and South Australia. How fortunate that those two States happened to lie next to each other; it did mean that in the old days there was one state boundary which was not also a break-of-gauge point. So, to this day the 3ft 6in gauge lines of Western Australia and Queensland, particularly the latter, have smaller and lighter equipment not only than other Australian railways, but also than many other 3ft 6in gauge lines in other parts of the world; 'narrow-gauge,' a dismissive pejorative, summed them up. It is tactless to remark that (although heavy-duty mineral lines are a special case) even now they are more productive and economical, that the gross deficit per ton-mile of Australian railways gets larger as the rails go farther apart. Only an insensitive, coarse, and old-fashioned hack will bother to point this out. A bright and forward-looking author will instead pick up his typewriter and say (entirely truthfully) 'The "Indian-Pacific," one of the most modern and comfortable passenger trains in the world, runs directly through from Perth to Sydney (2500 miles). Its space is normally sold out weeks in advance; since it started to run in 1969, it has become a national institution.'

Right:
The Hawkesbury River Bridge on the main line between Sydney and Melbourne.

Right, bottom:
A new double-deck electric long-distance train set in Sydney Central station.

Below:
A class BB 18¼ 4–6–0 heads a local Queensland passenger train.

Route 17
Perth to the Bluff

The 'Indian-Pacific' is indeed a classic train. It is beautiful to look at. There is something about heavy, handsome, comfortable stainless-steel coaches, gliding along on great coil-sprung bogies, somnolent occupants glimpsed in their air-conditioning through tinted glass windows. The feeling of envy is somewhat enhanced if one is standing, hot and dusty, by the lineside. Like other luxury trains, one buys space on the 'Indian-Pacific' not transport. It is like a hotel which happens to move. If one wants nowadays simply to get from Perth to Sydney, just as if one wants to cross any other continent, one flies. Fortunately enough people in Australia want to ride the train to make it morally worthwhile running it even if not quite financially.

The rolling stock of the train is American, of the type of the last full-flowered period of train travel in that nation in the late 1940s. Perhaps more exactly the 'Indian-Pacific' goes one step better – what Budd or Pullman-Standard might have been building by the late 1950s if orders for new passenger trains had kept coming. However, the 'Indian-Pacific' stock was built in the late 1960s, after nearly all the American trains it was modelled on had ceased to exist. In this sense it is possible to say that there has never been another train like it.

Nowadays one blasts across Australia, on one gauge all the way, direct via Broken Hill and the Nullarbor Plains: 2500 miles in 65 hours (approximately). Australia's railways are not built for speed; curves and grades and light track compel otherwise. The transcontinental line is now much improved and the days when one drummed across the desert, stony pancake-flat to every horizon, straight as an arrow at a limit of 45mph are gone. Nowadays it is more likely to be 55–60mph. Still, the first part of the route from Perth, the 400-mile section to Kalgoorlie, nowadays has the fastest passenger trains in the country, some railcars of a luxuriousness to match that of the 'Indian-Pacific' itself, which maintain an end-to-end average of around a mile a minute. One might do worse than take one of these, and break one's journey overnight. Today mining has moved away from Kalgoorlie, but the old town has kept something of the turn-of-the-century gold-rush atmosphere. Otherwise, there is not a great deal to be said about the journey. The stunning thing about what one sees out of the window is how similar it all is; there

can be few train journeys anywhere in the world which offer so little scenic variety. There are, however, parts of Australia, even of Western Australia, which are beautiful; and there are railways in Australia which rate high in visual interest. It is nonetheless unfortunate that the transcontinental run does not go near any of the first, or over any of the second. The scenic high spot, in fact, is the crossing of the Blue Mountains, just beyond the limit of Sydney's western suburbs.

All this may sound pretty dismissive of what is still undeniably a very fine train. Train travelling in Australia provides rewards in other ways: one's involvement with one's fellow-passengers, and the experience of seeing something of one of the world's most incredible landscapes. Australia's landscape is so big and so empty, and yet here and there supports a small scale of civilized life so strangely satisfactorily, that the journey does turn out to have a worthwhile point to it. Getting the flavor of a land so unusual – the last frontier of the west – makes it worth spending a few days on a journey which could be 'jetted' in a few hours.

In steam days the transcontinental passenger service was rather differently organized. Until the late 1950s the competition was not from the air, but from the sea; Australia's main cities are all on the coast and were traditionally linked by ship. The liners which plied between Melbourne and Perth were pleasant and reliable. The rail service followed as nearly as possible the same route, curving southwards to pass through Adelaide and Melbourne instead of taking the short cut across via Broken Hill. This did not then reduce the number of breaks-of-gauge; but the shorter route was so lightly-built and slow that it was quicker to go 200 miles further and get some heavier rail under the wheels. The 2700 miles took about 84 hours overall, but this included a business day in Melbourne on the way; so the 32mph overall average speed was not really much slower than now. One did, of course, have to keep changing; from 3ft 6in to standard gauge at Kalgoorlie, to 5ft 3in at Port Pirie, and back to standard at Albury (which was usually near or after midnight). But the trains had variety as well as some style. The writer remembers watching the transcontinental express leaving Perth about

Left:
In Australia's Victoria State 4–6–2s R701 and R705 head an enthusiasts' special train as it passes Heathcote Junction.

Extreme left and below:
The 'Indian Pacific' express near Port Augusta in South Australia.

25 years ago, behind a newish, vastly noisy, and very smelly diesel. It was one of the first main-line diesels in Western Australia; the WAGR were so displeased with them they returned to steam and had another batch of 2–8–2s built, which proved a better investment as they outlived those first diesels. However, the machine in question achieved motion on that occasion. It was a long train, of turn-of-the-century stylish twelve-wheeled wooden-bodied coaches; in its own way it radiated comfort and opulence just as the 'Indian-Pacific' does now, even if one seemed to hear the creaking of some of the bodywork above the noise of the wheels. There was white paint and polished brass, plenty of customers inside just getting themselves settled, and the famous piano in the observation – bar car at the back. And that is a tradition that has been kept; only Australian trains have pianos.

The 'Indian Pacific' express on the trans-Australian Railway.

An extreme example can still be typical and in that kind of way the 'Indian-Pacific' is perhaps typical of Australian long-distance rail travel. Over the very long distances, there never was a golden age of opulent comfort. There was too little traffic ever to have supported it; the wonder was that the rails got there, nevermind the trains which ran on them. But all the same, there was a surprisingly strong effort to keep standards high. To this day the total service on the line to Alice Springs, in the middle of the continent, is one mixed train a week. It is, admittedly, one of the very few mixed trains in the world with an official name (the 'Ghan,' after the Afghan camel-drivers who inaugurated service on the route), and has a sleeping and a dining car.

Fairly sweeping cuts have begun to be made in passenger rail services in some areas, including most of Western Australia and a large segment of

New South Wales, which for a long time resisted branch line closures better than most places. But with passenger flows on this remote Australian scale, the bus is an undeniably better tool than the train, if you leave the car and the airplane out of the reckoning. Yet it is surprising how much train service remains, some of quite an off-beat nature. Along the coastal strip from Adelaide to Northern Queensland, where most Australians live, there are some excellent, well-maintained, reliable trains. One can readily travel in modern, comfortable stock, with dining and sleeping cars, over any part of this route of nearly 3000 miles and still on all three gauges. And the break-of-gauge points are now no longer on the state borders, but in Melbourne and Brisbane.

This account began by rejecting one journalist's cliché about Australian railways, which has, just the same, dogged the reader ever since. It is time to reject another just as firmly. All writers about Australia tend to emphasize the vast, remote outback. But however, this is not where most Australians live; Australia is an urban country, and when its city-dwellers go out, they usually go to its gorgeous beaches. Most Australian passenger trains, therefore, are urban ones, mainly electric multiple-units, chasing each other down multi-track lines on close headways. It is difficult to think of a European city which, for its size, is so congested with buzzing, complex, commuter railways as Melbourne. But it is also difficult to think of one which still runs, alongside some sound modern equipment, such antiquated wooden-bodied trains. Perhaps New York is the nearest comparison. It is all a very rare mixture; there is nothing quite like the Australian railway scene anywhere else in the world.

Below:
Class D3 4–6–0 and class R 4–6–2 on special trains for steam enthusiasts near Malvern, Australia.

Bottom:
The 'Western Endeavour' was the first and only steam train to travel across the Australian continent between Sydney and Perth.

New Zealand

Australia and New Zealand are 'black and white'; they really have nothing in common, apart from language and what some people regard as close geographical proximity. In fact, Sydney and Wellington are about as distant from each other as Paris is from Naples, Stockholm from Athens, or Montreal from Miami. New Zealand is cooler, wetter, more fertile, more various, more beautiful and above all, smaller. The railways are narrow gauge (3ft 6in), but again have nothing in common with the frail Australian systems of the same width. New Zealanders have always set about doing what was needed, which involved running more and heavier trains faster. Their physical performance has always been comparable with the best Australian standard-gauge, and their economic performance has always been better. But this applies chiefly to the freight side of the business. Australian railways have, as mentioned earlier, always laid themselves out to improve their passengers' lot as much as possible, and still maintain this tradition. The NZGR, on the other hand, was delighted to use the war as an excuse to abolish dining-car service in 1917 and never, while the steam age lasted, brought it back; by 1945 it had pretty well stopped trying with its still fairly brisk and presentable passenger trains, and proceeded for the next 25 years to try to strangle any remnants. Success was not as great as the management hoped, and ultimately there was a reaction. The present NZR runs a very small number of long-distance passenger trains and, on the whole, those which it does run are very good at holding their own against an equally excellent internal airline system. *And* the dining car has returned.

In the North Island, both Auckland and Wellington have a suburban train network. The former is rather under-used; although Auckland is twice as large as Wellington, its development has grown *away* from the tracks. In a rather similar way, what long-distance services there are radiate from Wellington; lines going in other directions from Auckland are all now freight-only. Nowadays the Auckland-Wellington main line has three daily passenger services: a fast all-sleeper overnight train, very modern and comfortable in rather the new Australian style, with a shower in each berth; a rather slower overnight maid-of-all-work train, with chair cars only (but also a diner); and a rather remarkable high-speed Japanese-built railcar which does the run by daylight. All these trains had steam-age equivalents, but the day train ran only during the brief summer holiday peak, whereas its successor runs year-round.

Most long-distance railcars anywhere are rather purgatorial, tending to be hot, noisy, and bouncy. Certainly this was the case with the majority of such vehicles in New Zealand, which administered the *coup de grâce* to many country passenger services. But the three units which now cover this

Oil-fired class Ka 4–8–4 No 238 powers the New Zealand Wellington-Auckland express in 1955.

Auckland-Wellington day service called the 'Silver Fern,' are a revelation, and among the most comfortable trains the writer has ever ridden. They are fast, silent, air-conditioned and smooth-riding most of the way – much of the sharply-curved track in the mountainous center of the island has been battered and dog-legged by the heavy freights. Even though long stretches are limited to around 40mph the sideways 'bang' at every railjoint is quite fierce. But on better-aligned sections these railcars demonstrate what can be done. With the evidently accurate speedo-meter needle hard against the stop beyond 120kph, they show silken-smooth riding, that the 3ft 6in gauge is perfectly all right, and that what counts more is the quality of the engineering.

The journey is scenically pleasant, and becomes majestic in the high country as the train winds past two semi-retired snowcapped volcanoes and over a succession of dramatically high steel trestles. A hostess comes along from time to time with coffee and sandwiches but there is a limit to what can be done in a two-car unit about full meals. Instead the post-1917 NZR tradition of the mealtime stop has been maintained in this one instance, to allow a knees-under-the-table lunch. And to be fair to the NZR, its Refreshments Branch got quite adept at funnelling good plain cooking into a train-load of customers, quite pleasantly, in double-quick time.

The only inter-island ferry service nowadays

runs from Wellington to Picton; it takes a couple of hours to cross Cook Strait followed by nearly as long a time steaming up the long, narrow fjord to the railhead at Picton. The ferries, operated by the NZR, are combined rail- and road-vehicle carriers, with passengers considered rather as an afterthought. They are even more liable than the trains to be booked-out at holiday times. Assuming one gets aboard, and given fine weather, it is a delightful passage. But be warned about the weather; this is one of the most 'lively' crossings in the world at times.

The North and South Islands of New Zealand

are entirely different in landscape; the North is mountainous, but except for the three great volcanic peaks by no means alpine. The South Island is rugged from end to end, broken only by the plains sloping down to the east coast in the central part, and glaciated rolling hills in the far south. From north to south, the Southern Alps are crossed by only one railway and five roads, all that link the east and west coasts in 500 miles. Thus the traveller sees quite a different country from Australia, and one with smaller towns and a slower pace of life.

The 218-mile Christchurch to Picton line, in fact, did for a time lose all its passenger trains. Following the senescence of the railcar fleet, the service was taken off for a couple of years. Finally it was restored, using ex-railcars refurbished and de-engined, and turned into a proper train with a diesel to pull it and a luggage van at the back. To enable one train instead of two to cover the line, on an out-and-home run leaving Christchurch early in the morning, the schedule now connects at Picton with the ferry to and from Wellington, which the previous service never did; consider-

able numbers of passengers have begun to use it. It is a fine ride, through a country wild and deserted enough to pass for Australia, but spectacular as well. An even more beautiful journey is to make a side-trip from Christchurch across to the West Coast at Greymouth, a service still worked by the last surviving railcars at the time of writing. The line climbs up past snowy peaks, across spindly viaducts, and along chasms rocky enough to meet the most demanding Colorado standards. At the summit it passes through the 5.25-mile long Otira tunnel, once the longest in the British Empire. But, in the last 25 years, line changes have caused the building of two more, each slightly longer, in the North Island.

The only other long-distance passenger train service in the South Island is on the main line, from Christchurch through Dunedin to Invercargill, 369 miles. The daily express was in fact the last job scheduled for steam locomotives on the NZR, for several years after diesels had taken over everything else. It has now been smartened up and accelerated as well as dieselized, covering the distance in some 10 hours (which is good considering that half the run is far from straight and level, indeed for 50 miles north of Dunedin quite difficult). One might notice that the overall speed is about the same as the 'Indian-Pacific.' The coaches are old but rebuilt and modernized, and once again there is a dining car; the 'Southerner' is a very respectable train.

The short, flat branch from Invercargill to Bluff (17 miles) is the southernmost *public* railway in the world (the Argentinians have built the famous but *non-public* 2ft 6in gauge to the collieries at Rio Turbio in Southern Patagonia). The journey to Bluff nowadays has to be made by road, because (provided one made the Greymouth diversion, and while in Greymouth travelled on the nine-mile branch to Rewanui, a colliery with no road access) by the time one has reached Invercargill one has travelled over all the railways in the South Island which offer passenger service – with one exception. During the summer (Christmas to Easter) the NZR operates its last steam locomotives on the tourist service from Lumsden to Kingston (38 miles) in the Southern Lake District. This is certainly a train for the collector; although it cannot claim to be the world's southernmost steam train (since the Rio Turbio line is emphatically all-steam) it is certainly the southernmost steam *passenger* train.

Left:
A Japanese-built 1050 hp class Dj diesel electric locomotive leaves Wellington, New Zealand on a test run.

Below:
New Zealand's old Rimutaka incline – note the raised center rail; the special locomotives shown were fitted with horizontal driving wheels which gripped this rail. The system enabled traction to be maintained on the 1 in 12 gradient.

171

Southeast Asia

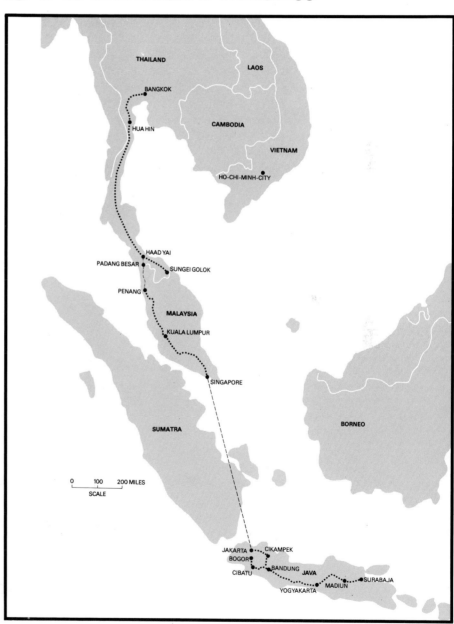

In pre-war – colonial – days, railways in Southeast Asia had generally a good press. In part this was certainly because the area was, and remains, one of the most favored and beautiful corners of the globe; here there was wealth and population enough to enable the job to be done in style. But in the other part some of the image was in the style itself, which to a degree reflected the railroad practise and flavor of the colonial power. Exiled rubber planters in Malaya, for instance, naturally would give the Federated Malay States Railways bonus points for being as much as possible a tropical meter-gauge replica of the Great Western Railway back home. And so it was, give or take the jungles, the palm trees, and a fleet of poppet-valved Pacifics. In design these last might have been as unSwindonian as conveniently possible, but they were painted Brunswick Green and had copper-capped chimneys;

the coaches were chocolate and cream, the signals pure GWR, and so on. Similarly, in Indo-China the French imposed a style of railwaying which was purely that of metropolitan France, though fortunately and despite the fragmented character of the network in those days, the model was metropolitan French main line, reduced in proportion to the meter gauge, and not (as in Madagascar for example) a straight copy of metropolitan French rural light railway. Burma was colonized at one remove, not so much by Britain as by British India, and the Burmese Railways were hardly distinguishable from Indian meter-gauge standard practise. Thailand, on the other hand, was never colonized at all (its very name means 'Land of the Free'), and so the Royal State Railways could choose and mix their influences instead of having to drink only out of one bottle. On the whole this tended to mean British

A Malaysian special vintage steam train with preserved oil-fired poppet valve 4–6–2 locomotive.

signalling and American locomotives, a judicious pair of choices.

Which leaves the Dutch, in Java and Sumatra, as the odd men out, which they succeeded in becoming to some purpose. The Javanese railways, in particular, had developed a very strong character of their own by 1941. The Dutch railwaymen revelled in doing all the things they could not do in their small, flat homeland, and faced with long distances and mountain grades, tunnels and spindly steel trestles, all in rich and densely populated country, exploded into a coruscation of compound Pacifics, Mallets, twelve-coupled tanks, zigzags and horseshoes, complex networks, and unique signalling variations. It all added up to what was unquestionably the finest narrow-gauge (3ft 6in) system in the world by the 1930s, and the only one which ran regularly at 70mph.

The war, and political upheavals afterwards, changed all that. Vietnam is a story known to all, but the railways of Burma and Indonesia suffered almost as much in earlier days, in each case for the same reason, that the new independent governments could not find any meaning or direction once the anti-colonialist struggle had been won. Political posturings became the order of the day, coupled with a move akin to rejecting the problems of the real world in favor of a return to the simple securities of the nursery, by inventing and confronting non-existent 'neo-colonial' exploitations. In this dreamland, organizing the maintenance or improvement of one's own state railway system became a boring drudge, and thus a lost cause, along with much else in the way of sewerage, hospitals, education, and so on. No folly ever runs quite unchecked forever, and in Indonesia these particular follies are now being remedied.

Surabaja is a teeming city and great port, with all the infrastructure of a great trade center. The telephones work as well as in Paris, the electricity is as reliable as in Sofia, the roads are paved as well as on Manhattan. The people are a great deal friendlier than in any of those other cities; indeed, on the journey to Bangkok by rail in the 1970s the writer took great pleasure and interest in his fellow travellers. The trains, however, were not what they had been, but that did not matter.

The typical Javanese long-distance train today is made up of relatively modern and very spartan steel coaches, built in East Germany, hauled by a West German diesel-hydraulic or possibly an American diesel-electric. Except on a few trains, only third class is offered, with seat spacing more suited for the lightly-built Javanese than bulky Europeans; fortunately overcrowding is not so universal as it was. However even third-class-only trains will somehow manage to provide food en route; a small squad mainly of young women based in one compartment or in a corner of the van will contrive to produce and bring to the passenger a hot and tasty variety of rice dishes, or if preferred, one can buy food at most stations on the way. Night travel means sitting up, but trains are reasonably frequent and if one has time one can choose to break one's journey and stay in a hotel. Or it is possible to cover the 500 or so miles from Surabaja to Jakarta in a single day's run by starting at the crack of dawn (4.55 am). (By Javanese standards this is not particularly early in the morning; most people will have already started work.)

Of several days spent on the journey, a series of memory-images remain. There was a large area of green, almost empty, space which was once the marshalling yard between Surabaja (Gubeng) and Wonokromo, the main junction just outside the city; the sidings could be seen still undulating through the grass. There was a big Krupp 2–8–2 leaning over at a drunken angle, seemingly off the rails, but apparently not. A series of astonishingly high, vast, volcanic cone-shaped mountains, each standing well clear of the next, set the scene for a series of steam locomotive depots full of the most remarkable antiques, some still in action, including the 90-year-old 2–4–0s at Madiun, one of them converted to burn oil (or more accurately tar) which it was doing rather noisily, with deep intestinal pops and rumbles. A series of friendly fellow-passengers tried out their English, often quite comprehensibly. A long unexplained wait in the open country ended as we eased closely past a derailed oil tank wagon on a siding, still coupled to a little steam streetcar engine about a third its size but still on the rails. A tourist 'must' is to complete the circuit round the Sultan's palace at Yogyakarta, marble and corrugated iron, treasure and tinsel, still guarded by the Sultan's enormously aged but still warlike and dignified private soldiers. Not much steam locomotion was visible by day, but beautiful chime whistles could be heard by night. The friezes on the wall of the dining room of the old colonial hotel next to the station (not quite outclassed) portrayed the Dutch, with affection, through Javanese eyes.

The line now went on to Bandung on a secondary route through the mountains. There was more stunning scenery, but the countryside was becoming more densely populated all the time. Rice paddies could be seen terraced high up the hillside – no irrigatable fertile soil could be wasted. One small hillock in the valley below, perhaps 30ft high and 100ft in diameter at the base, had all been terraced, with water led to its summit by a crazy conduit of bamboo poles tied together. One then passes through Cibatu, the last and only place in the world with a steam locomotive depot all of whose allocation were articulated types (but mostly out of service). Bandung is a small hill town, high enough to be cool and comfortable for administrative types before air-conditioning. The railway station there is large and empty with a new and prestigious modern power signal-box; but nowadays there are too few trains to justify it. The daily train to Bogor, on the old original line to Jakarta, consisted of no coaches, no vans, no trucks, just one very run-down 2–8–2T pulling another one, dead and rodless, but with passengers sitting all over it and with 1 in 25 grades ahead, clearly loaded with all the weight it could haul. (When departure time came and the driver opened the regulator, the crosshead on the side of the engine

next to me jumped half an inch before the main crankpin started, and then the driving axle sloggered forward in the worn-out horns and boxes another inch at least before the engine began to move.)

From Bandung to Jakarta, 110 miles, is one of the better and more rehabilitated lines, with some trains doing the run in the respectable time of 2½ hours, including long stretches at a genuine 70mph once the double-track north coast main line has been joined west of Cikampek. The great swooping curves of the new descent out of the hills is also impressive; this must have been a fine line in steam days. Jakarta, the capital, is something like Surabaja but much more hectic and very much more crowded. Flimsy houses encroach up to the very sleeper ends; indeed some were obviously built straight on top of disused, or insufficiently used, tracks. One large marshalling yard at Tanahabang had (at the time of the author's travels) simply become a tented city, with vans and boxcars standing here and there still on the rails but obviously marooned for years. Most of them had one (or several) families living in the van body, and more between the wheels, no doubt at a lower rental. Such pressure of population traditionally means squalor, filth, disease, poverty; squalor there was, and some evident disease, but much less than I would have expected, and the crowds of eager children were friendly and looked healthy and well-fed. Despite its woes, Java is a rich land; which is the message put across more clearly, but less convincingly, in the clean, spacious, modern, international hotel quarter nearby.

Jakarta to Singapore is an hour by jet or a day by ship, but a much greater distance apart in style and politics which is strange considering how much the two cities have traditionally had in common, even a shared language (Malay on the north side of the straits, Bahasa Indonesia on the south). The fact that Singapore is now predominantly a Chinese city explains the difference much more than the old and vanishingly relevant distinction between British and Dutch colonial styles. There is not much left of the British presence in Singapore, or perhaps the British legacy has been assimilated. The greatest memorial to the past is the monumental city center, built in the pride of the empire on which the sun never set (until January 1942). But the buildings are still used, cleaned and cared for.

The railways of Malaysia, which begin at Singapore, may be much better preserved than those of Java but they clearly were never, in the old days, meant to be in the same class at all. One need only compare the exit from Tanjung Priok, the port, through Jakarta, by way of a warren of flying junctions and multiple tracks, all electrified, with the casual way in which the two plat-

A magnificent 2–6–6–0 Mallet locomotive of the Indonesian State Railways.

forms of Singapore station in a few yards have narrowed down to a single meter-gauge track which corkscrews off apologetically between and entirely ignored by the houses pressing in on either side. Scenically, the run from Singapore to Bangkok has not a fraction of the interest of the Javanese countryside. The Malaysian peninsula in particular as seen from the railway tracks, consists of jungle and more jungle, interrupted by clearings where things happen – towns, farms and tin mines. Mountains are often visible but never very close. In steam days there were two passenger trains: the 'Day Mail' and the 'Night Mail.' One started after breakfast and kept going until it got there about 'tiffin' time; the other started in the early evening and had usually arrived by the time it got properly light. This schedule could be applied, for instance, to the run from Singapore to Kuala Lumpur, some 300 miles. Diesels and speed-ups have created a third train, a lightweight flyer, which leaves about noon and arrives not long after the 'Day Mail.' It might not have been a bad mistake to travel on this 'flyer' if the Australian-built railcar scheduled for the turn had performed, but it often does not and the scratch train was made up of some none-too-salubrious

hard-seated third-class coaches that rode much worse than Javanese ones, despite similar speeds on better track. Worst of all was haulage by a diesel which seemed to pour out its exhaust at window level. Passengers bounced up the length of Malaysia, from Singapore to Penang, in a dense and suffocating miasma of poison gas – not, regrettably, a very pleasant journey. Admittedly, the splendid station at Kuala Lumpur, minarets at each platform end, a slightly tarnished mini-Taj Mahal with Venetian overtones, still charmed but it would have been dazzling if not seen through diesel smog. Having endured enough by the time he reached Penang, the author chose to cross the Thai border to Haad Yai by bus.

Haad Yai is a small town over 600 miles south of Bangkok by rail; it is linked with the main landmass of Asia by the fairly narrow Kra isthmus. One imagines a long, rather ramshackle, certainly lightly used, meter-gauge single track when looking at the map, and the impression was reinforced by the Malaysian timetable which showed a train running north from Penang to the Thai border at Padang Besar, with through coaches for Bangkok, only three days a week. But the facts are otherwise. So far as the Thais are con-

A modern diesel-hauled train running from Haad Yai to Butterworth in Malaysia.

cerned, Penang (and Singapore) are on a branch line; most of their rail traffic serves the fertile area along the northeast coast between Haad Yai and the other crossing of the Malaysian border at Sungei Golok, and four or five quite good express trains make the 20–24-hour run every day. These are now all diesel-hauled, and dining and sleeping cars can be found. But this area of Thailand saw the last stand of steam locomotives, and from the overbridge at Haad Yai station could be seen no fewer than 14 Pacifics and 2–8–2s moving around the large and quite modern yard. Within a few minutes another gleaming 4–6–2 rolled smartly into the station with a 12-coach crowded passenger train which was the daily all-stations local from Sungei Golok. Even at this stage of dieselization, most of the distance to Bangkok could still be travelled behind steam power by using a series of local trains like this one. Thus that is how one could go, taking advantage of the breaks of journey by spending a day or two at a couple of delightful seaside hotels on the way, most notably the old railway-owned inn at Hua Hin, developed when the Thai royal family took up golf; it has an excellent golfcourse, a marvellous beach plus a beautifully ornate royal waiting room at the station.

The journey was interesting enough from the railway point of view and a very energetic performance, good to see and hear, from the locomotive as it accelerated the heavy train away from a stop every five or six miles and up to a steady line speed of 45–50mph. There was more scenic variety than in Malaysia, if less than in Java. This railway line was clearly the main means of access to all the towns and villages around; at each stop jeeps and buses exchanged passengers with us. At one place the train connected with a motorboat, propelled in the standard Thai manner by a car engine on one end of a balanced pole handled by the steersman, the other end bearing a propeller. With 30 or 40 passengers on board, the boat roared off into the distance at a surprising speed down a canal, perhaps eight feet wide.

Tourists are not common on trains such as this one, generally preferring to take one of the expresses mentioned earlier. The author found himself the object of considerable polite curiosity and in spite of severe language barriers, conversed (in sign language) more than adequately with local Thais. Eventually passengers and train arrived at Bangkok.

An eight-coach push-pull diesel express arriving at Bangkok station.

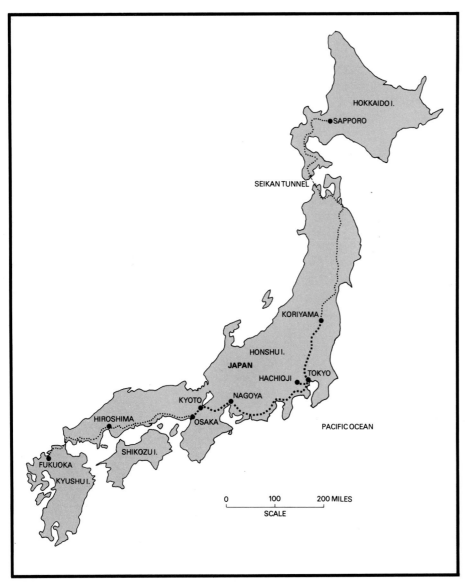

Japan had to offer in the way of railways whether they were connected with the FOCS (Freight Operations Control System) or otherwise.

Actually, the program that the Japanese National Railways had arranged would suit anyone very well for a short visit to Japan. One went early one morning to see the unbelievable sight of white-gloved people-packers pressing customers into JNR's elegant Tokyo suburban trains at Shinjuku – certainly one of the railway wonders of the world. But, of course, what the author was waiting for was his first experience of land transport at over 100mph start-to-stop, rare enough even today – in 1968 such a thing was a unique wonder. The most impressive thing about the ride was its unimpressiveness – almost none of the expected sensations of speed was experienced except that 123 minutes after leaving Tokyo he stepped out onto the platforms at Nagoya, 229 miles away.

After Nagoya there was Osaka, then the farthest place one could go in the 'bullet trains.' Nowadays one can travel on in them via Hiroshima and the longest undersea tunnel in the world to Fukuoka on Kyushu Island. High speed is achieved in difficult country by building the

With some of the greatest railway engineering on earth to their credit, the Japanese National Railways, in spite of festering problems in some areas, are certainly among the world leaders in the field. The famous 'Shin Kansen' or 'Bullet Train' railway is envied the world over – who else offers overall average speeds by rail well over 100mph on a main line more than 700 miles long, with six express trains leaving the main terminal every hour? Such is train service between Tokyo, Osaka and Fukuoka.

You can imagine how pleased the writer was to accompany a group of professional railwaymen assigned to study what the Japanese had done in the way of developing computerized methods of controlling freight movements. A serious subject, of course, but it did not prevent us enjoying other things that Japanese National Railways (and Japan) had to offer.

Route 19
People-
Packers,
Bullet Trains
and Fiery
Dragons

Business travellers today, even when on railway business, are not, alas, permitted such indulgences as a ride on the trans-Siberian railway, but at least, on the author's great-circle course over the North Pole to Tokyo, he did not over-fly any railways except Uncle Sam's Alaska Railroad. On arrival it was at once made clear that, like it or not, he was going to be shown everything

extension line almost straight (the sharpest curve is 2½ miles radius), at the expense of 139 miles of tunnelling and 73 miles of bridging. This leaves a mere 35 miles of ordinary railway. Odd to think that if one took the normal train (which also runs the full distance) back to Tokyo, the 736-mile journey would take 16½ hours overnight instead of seven hours.

Before returning to Tokyo, the delegation spent a weekend at Kyoto in a traditional Japanese-style hotel. It is probably enough to say that these establishments provide slippers, dressing-gown, pyjamas, razor and toothbrush but no beds, chairs and nothing other than a communal bath. Of course, Western-style hotels also exist in the main cities.

As well as the famous and beautiful temples and sacred gardens located near Nara, one can visit the locomotive shed at Umekoji roundhouse in Kyoto. Many 4–6–2s ('Pacifics') and 2–8–2s (called 'Mikados' – 'Mikes' for short – because the type was first built for and supplied to Japan) are present. (In fact, a Pacific rolled into the station with a local passenger train, just as our guide, who came from headquarters, was saying that there were no such things in Japan any more.) Umekoji is now, in fact, a living shrine to the steam locomotive, which is worshipped as passionately in Japan as anywhere in the world; many of the locomotives now held at Kyoto are in running order, although nothing is known in definitive terms regarding any program of excursions.

Back in Tokyo, we were told the story of the English engineer who was in charge of building the first railway in Japan. It is said that he made a special point of teaching his Japanese staff the elements of survey and construction, so that they should not in future be dependent on foreigners. The fact that he had married a beautiful Japanese girl may have had something to do with it. This seemed an appropriate point to ask the favor of a day out with steam....

A few days later, therefore, the writer found himself, dressed according to the rules in a Japanese engine-driver's uniform – which must have been specially made since he is a good head and shoulders taller than most Japanese – drinking green tea with the shed-master at Hachioji roundhouse, situated north of Tokyo, near the limit of the suburban area. Introduction to the driver and fireman (formal exchange of visiting

A Japanese National Railways' high-speed train on the new Tokaido Line. Mount Fuji is in the background.

cards with both) of 2–8–2 locomotive D 51–1151 followed and soon enough this clean and well-maintained iron horse was swinging out of the yards with its load of freight.

A railwayman from Britain felt quite at home on a railway system with left-hand running on rail (and road, too), as well as stations with high-level platforms; once the main line was left for secondary metals, archetypal British pattern semaphore signals were added and, as we entered a single-line section, the signalman handed up a thing in a leather pouch – with a loop to catch it with – to the fireman. 'In Japanese (said the interpreter) we call that a *tab-let*.'

The glories of the 'Bullet Trains' on the new Tokaido Line tend to obscure superb and presently un-matched running on the 3ft 6in gauge. The party visited what was mysteriously called a 'Cybernetic Island' (otherwise a heavily computerized marshalling yard) at Koriyama, 142 miles northeast of Tokyo, travelling out and back (at an average speed of 53mph and a maxi-mum of 75mph) in the day using high-speed narrow-gauge electric express trains.

It was permitted to travel in the cab, high up in a dome above normal roof level and far above the so-close-together rails, listening to the assistant driver calling the 'all-clear' to his mate every time he saw a green signal – no other kind was seen.

While cab rides are something not normally made available to a tourist, there was a debit side which has left more than a tinge of regret. This was because the exigencies of the work to be done made it impossible to go further north and cross by train-ferry on to Hokkaido Island, where at that time there was much steam, including triple-headed 4–6–4s on the principal express to Sapporo as well, of course, as superb skiing. However, the reader will soon be able to make this journey by high-speed train, via the amazing 33-mile undersea Seikan tunnel, which at long last will wrest from London Transport's Northern Line the world record for the longest rail tunnel.

Extreme right, top:
A Japanese National Railways' standard class D51 2–8–2 locomotive pulls a freight train at Hachioji Junction.

Below:
A Japanese National Railways' 3ft 6in gauge express train. These are the fastest narrow-gauge trains in the world, running at speeds up to 75mph.

China

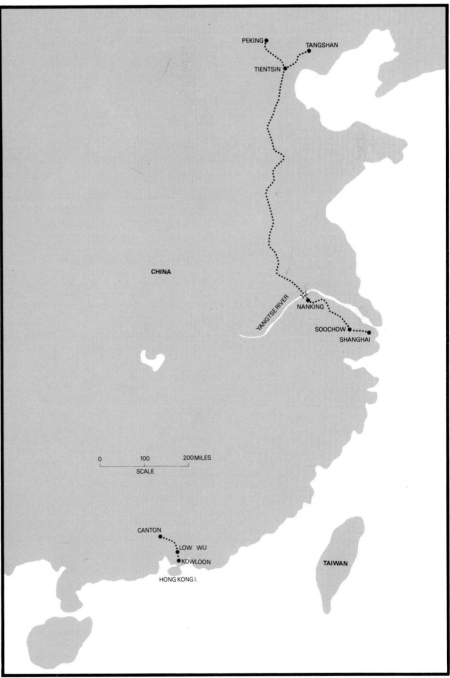

Route 20
The Steamy Rails of China

Chinese Railways, like Chinese politics, have remained very much an enigma to Western eyes. After many years of trying, the 'To Europe For Steam' organization succeeded in obtaining a visit there, which on arrival turned out to be only 20 percent railways (19 percent steam railways, though) and 80 percent other things.

The Chinese frontier was reached by train from Hong Kong, and it was with some apprehension that we crossed on foot the covered railway bridge leading into the People's Republic. In the event, it was an apprehension that proved to be groundless, for the Immigration and Customs arrangements included armchair seats instead of line-ups and a free and delicious lunch.

Furthermore, it very soon became apparent that the Chinese are no more sensitive to the photography of locomotives and trains than of handcarts, provided – in either case – no big bridge is involved (except, oddly, the biggest of all, the Yangtse River bridge at Nanking, which is apparently a showpiece) or anything military or under construction. Nevertheless, there was a problem. Parties visiting China are expected to regard themselves as privileged and to take their trip very seriously indeed. This means the study of Chinese society at first hand, and while not perhaps from the cradle to the grave, certainly from factory crèche to old persons home! In fact, only one-fifth of our planned visit involved railways. True, the 05.30–07.30 period each morning was usually available for do-it-yourself expeditions, but difficulties nevertheless arose because unescorted and unannounced tourists cannot gain access to station platforms, while good photographic locations away from stations are hard to find in city environments.

There was no deliberate attempt to ignore the party's expressed wish to see as much of the railways as possible; it was more that the whole concept of amateur railway enthusiasm is totally incomprehensible to the Chinese – as indeed it is to many Western people! Convinced therefore that a group which had only a few actual railwaymen among its members could not possibly want an undiluted diet of railways, they gave us a program with a modest railway content. We met nothing but the greatest courtesy and friendliness in homes, schools, farms and factories. The hotels were fine and the food simple but good in the Chinese tradition, and after a day or two the party took to chopsticks as to the manner born.

From the steam enthusiasts' point of view, all this might seem to add up to total disaster, but it was not so. For a start, the other parts of our program were almost always fascinating and in any case, when we did get near the railways, steam was usually very thick on the ground. In fact, except on the route between Kwangchow (Canton) and British territory at Hong Kong, which on both sides of the border is now totally diesel, anything but a steam-hauled freight was a rarity. Furthermore, the group was rather fortunate in that two of its six rail journeys were

steam-hauled, although the observed proportion of passenger trains so hauled was perhaps only half this.

It was almost exactly a week after take-off from Heathrow and four days after entering China that the party as a whole saw their first Chinese steam locomotive – during the course of an official tour of Peking station, built, amazingly, in under 12 months during 1959–60 as part of the 'Great Leap Forward.' Our pleasant but astute guides noted with astonishment the instant change of mood among the group from their usual manner of interested approval to unabashed ecstasy as we dashed across to Number 5 Platform where RM 'People' class 4–6–2 No 1250 had just arrived with an express.

Tall and handsome, this Pacific boasted $22\frac{1}{2} \times$ 26in cylinders, 5ft 10in wheels and 29,800lb tractive effort. Built in China in 1964, although noticeably different to anything any of us had

Right top:
A 'People' class RM 4–6–2 on passenger train at Tangshan.

Below right:
A 'People' class RM 4–6–2 locomotive at Peking Central Station.

seen before, it contained much from its Russian and American progenitors. It must be remembered that steam locomotive construction began in China at just about the time it was ceasing elsewhere, so it could be said that No 1250 was a nice example of average age. The class is the standard steam passenger type in China and in some ways is what a BR 'Britannia' might have looked like if, with similar axleload limitations, the designers had enjoyed an extra 36in of height to play with. All too soon, with a blast on her air horn, she was whisked away from us and the station visit proceeded in a calmer atmosphere.

The following day, having dutifully done such 'musts' as the Great Wall, the Forbidden City and the Metro during our stay, we left Peking, paying a second visit to the station but this time as travellers rather than people bent on finding what made it tick. (While on the subject of ticking,

incidentally, the clock on the great pagoda-roofed tower of Peking station chimes 'The East is Red' at noon and 6 pm!)

You can imagine our pleasure when, at a station where steam is only occasionally present, we saw a tender backing down on to our train, and moreover, when we discovered it was No 1250 again.

Out in the country, No 1250 used a steam chime whistle rather than the air horn and thus, ensconced in a soft-class sleeper in day use, located as second vehicle of the train, the party could delight in exhaust and whistle music and get cinders in its hair. And, perhaps, reflect how long it was since they had travelled in a steam train not by special arrangement but just by chance. For some it was the first time ever!

Tangshan came all too soon and the following day we were permitted to spend an hour or so on the station watching a parade of steam that no country, not even India or South Africa, could rival. One after another QJ 'Forward' class 2–10–2s kept rolling massive 2000-ton plus freight trains through on the main lines running, apparently, block-and-block all the time we were there. New JF 'Construction' and older JS 'Liberation' 2–8–2s were constantly on the move over the freight lines, while on the other side of the line was, awaiting delivery, a row of brand new SY 'Aiming High' class 2–8–2s. The whole added up to a feast of steam very much along the lines of what one imagines pre-war US railroading to have been. Or, perhaps, on reflection, Canadian, for while the array of old and new boxcars, gondolas and flats was completely North American, the uniformity of ownership was something only found in Commonwealth territory. If the sound of those chime whistles was anything to go by, this action continued day and night without pause for, make no mistake, China's railways are fully utilized.

The QJs, the current version of which has been constructed in China steadily since 1964, are big locomotives with $25\frac{1}{2} \times 31\frac{1}{2}$in cylinders, 59in wheels and 73,400lb tractive effort for a weight of 149 tons including tender. Older versions date back to 1956. A feature, common with the RM 4–6–2s and JS 2–8–2s, is an external steam pipe, contained in a massive casing, running forward from the dome to a regulator box on the smoke-box behind the chimney: this arrangement was typical of post-war Soviet designs, from which the Chinese built up their locomotive industry.

While in Tangshan, we visited a farming commune, and the journey there lay along a valley served by a brand new branch line. The trains we saw were hauled by equally new SYs, offering the amazing combination of newly built steam engines running on a newly laid branch line! On the third day, we left Tangshan, again by steam and this time we sampled lunch in the restaurant car. Chopsticks by now held no terrors for the party and this enabled us to enjoy a particularly nice meal in the Chinese style, simple but excellent.

We travelled as far as Tientsin, where we paused for a two-day stay, and during this time the only item of railway interest, the Civil Engineering Institute, did not involve trains or locomotives. The speed with which Chinese Railways are expanding (13,000 miles in 1950, 24,000 in 1970) is emphasized by the fact that some 140 Railway Civil Engineers graduate each year. Some amazing new railway projects, driven through the mountains in the west and south, have recently been completed and more are planned.

We left Tientsin in the evening for the 800-mile journey south to the ancient city of Soochow, giving 20 uninterrupted hours of undiluted railway enjoyment. As it turned out, the reality was even better than the prospect; although our own train was diesel-hauled, 95 percent of the locomotives we saw were steam. For a long time the types seen did not change, although their livery and embellishments showed great variety – not, I imagine, at the whim of individual drivers, for that would be against the philosophy of the regime, but possibly by decision of local revolutionary committees at each shed. Then all at once there was a click and things changed – we entered the land of the Flying Donkey!

The parade of QJ 2–10–2s we had been passing as we journeyed South suddenly gave way as we neared the Nanking area, to a rather different design classified (in this case, always in Roman characters) FD, but apparently without any patriotic class-name. These fine 2–10–2s had spoked rather than box-pok wheels, 12-wheel tenders instead of the usual eight and no external main steam pipe. In the absence of any official name, the group promptly christened them 'Flying Donkeys'; this was to the delight of the Chinese, because it subsequently transpired that they were ex-Russian FD Class engines. In full they are the 'Felix Dzherzhinsky' class, originally named after an early Chief of the Bolshevik secret police. Of 3200 built between 1931 and 1941, 2000 are reputed to have been sent to China during the 1950s involving conversion from 5ft to 4ft $8\frac{1}{2}$in gauge. The subsequent breach between China and Russia led to recriminations over the price – which we were told was 10 percent higher than the cost of building them new at home. After this, the originally chosen 'Friendship' classification seemed inappropriate, and they remained unnamed.

The crossing of the Yangtse River at Nanking marked the last stage of the journey and soon enough we reached Soochow, where the still extant and operative canal transportation system reminded us (just as it did Marco Polo) of Venice. Nothing of railway interest was shown to us here and, in fact, only one railway visit remained, although it turned out to be the best of all – a morning at the mechanized marshalling yard serving Shanghai. Although the equipment there was both modern and sophisticated, all movement, including humping, was steam-powered, with yet another class, the US-built KD 2–8–0s supplied under UNRAA auspices in 1946–47, predominating. Like the FDs, the KDs are regarded as 'imperialist' and therefore also unworthy of naming!

Apart from some KDs seen a day or so later in Kwangchow (Canton) – to which we flew by British-built Trident – this marshalling yard visit concluded our steam sightings.

We left China the way we had come, crossing on foot the railway bridge at Low Wu on the Canton-Kowloon railway, with the Red Flag flying at one end and the Union Jack at the other, noting as we did so the last six-bolt Chinese fishplate and the first British four-bolt one.

Just a tinge of regret remains for things we did not see, such as the Vulcan Foundry KF class 4–8–4s of 1937, the post-war 4–8–2s and 4–8–0s

supplied by Czechoslovakia and Hungary respectively to their standard designs, or the British ex-GWR Dean Goods 0–6–0s sent by UNRAA in 1946. Also believed to be around are the very large meter-gauge 2–8–8–2s supplied by the Americans in 1941 for the part-built China-Burma railway, streamlined 4–6–2s used in Manchuria before the war and a big-wheeled 2–8–4 (probably ex-Russian 'Joseph Stalin' type – the passenger version of the 'FD' 2–10–2) glimpsed in a photograph. The rumors of 4–12–4s in China would seem to be edging over into fantasy, but then so was the equally unbelievable rumor that steam locomotives were still in production. One might in conclusion observe that a country that can hide the Giant Panda in its forests, no doubt also has some railway mysteries.

Above:
A Chinese National Railways' dining car

Left:
The last class of steam locomotives to be built.

Index

Annex

Appendix

Addresses of organisations referred to in the text
Thomas Cook, Travel Agents & Timetable Publishers

    45 Berkeley St., London W1A 1EB

    587 Fifth Avenue, New York 10017

    435 North Michigan Avenue, Chicago, Illinois 60611

Dorridge Travel Services,

    7 Station Approach, Dorridge, Solihull, West Midlands, B93 8JA, England

Festiniog Travel

    The Harbour Station, Porthmadog, Gwynedd, North Wales

Intraflug A.G., for the Nostalgic ORIENT EXPRESS and other railway tours

    Tagernstrasse 12A, CH-8127 Forch, Zurich, Switzerland

Sea Containers Ltd., for the de-luxe vintage London–Venice Express

    1 Hanover Square, London W1

SARTOURS (for Steam Safaris in South Africa)

    48 Leicester Square, London W1

    610 Fifth Avenue, New York 10020

Southern Railway of USA passenger department (for steam excursions)

    First Federal Building, 40 Marietta St, N.W. Atlanta, Georgia 30324, USA

Steam Locomotive Operators Association of Britain,

    44 Stafford Rd., Litchfield, Staffordshire, England

To Europe For Steam (to everywhere for steam)

    22 Paddock Close, Quorn, Loughborough, Leicestershire, England

Travel Corporation of India

    Chander Mukhi, Nariman Point, Bombay 400021

Zillertal Railway

    Jenbach, Tirol, Austria

Acknowledgments

The author would like to thank those who helped him with this book. In particular his gratitude is due to Kenneth Mills for his South American contribution, Robert Tyrrell for his piece on Switzerland and John Snell for the Australasian and Indonesian chapters. Patrick Whitehouse of Basinghall Books was largely responsible for the picture research. A special word of thanks is due to Margot Cooper who typed out the manuscript.

Picture Credits

John Adams: 30. *C J Allen Collection:* 42 (bottom), 52/53 (both), 54/55, 56 (left 2), 79, 81 (top), 164/165. *Amtrak:* 51. *W J V Anderson:* 70, 105 (bottom). *Austrian Federal Railways:* 72/73. *BART:* 46 (bottom). *British Columbia Tourist Authority:* 58/59. *British Rail:* 26 (center). *Canadian Pacific:* 48 (bottom), 56/57. *Colourviews Collection:* 10, 11 (bottom), 12, 33 (both), 34/35, 63 (bottom right), 71 (top), 85 (bottom), 115, 171 (bottom). *Derek Cross:* 168/169. *D&RGW Railroad:* 49. *P Delacroix:* 95. *East African Railways:* 13. *J E Glover:* 24/25. *Harold A Edmonson:* 42/43. *Kevin Gould:* 132 (bottom left). *The Guardian:* 26 (bottom). *Emery J Gulash:* 38/39, 46/47 (top 3). *George Heiron:* 8/9, 29, 32, 36/37, 60/61. *Brian Hollingsworth:* 31 (bottom), 44/45, 48 (center), 69 (center right), 80/81, 102/103, 104 (center left), 146/147, 183 (top). *Everil Hollingsworth:* 6/7, 18/19, 82/83, 130/131, 132/133, 134/135, 136 (top), 138/139, 144 (center), 145 (both), 149 (center right), 154/155, 157 (bottom), 159 (bottom right). *Peter J. Howard:* 22/23, 27. *John Hunt:* 22/23, 27. *Bobby Jones:* 69 (bottom). *N R Knight:* 88 (center left). *Jack Lindsay:* 113 (top). *A Luft:* 73 (bottom right). *L Marshall:* 132 (center left), 136/137 (bottom), 140/141, 142/143, 144 (top), 147 (top right), 148/149. *Ken Mills:* 106/107, 108/109 (both), 110/111 (both), 112/113 (bottom 2), 116/117, 118/119 (top 2), 120/121, 122/123 (all 3), 124 (top left), 126/127 (all 3), 128/129. *John Moore:* 4/5, 9 (top), 40/41. *H Nave:* 69 (top). *New South Wales Government Railways:* 162/163. *Norwegian Railways:* 100/101, 104/105. *Shigeki Ohyama Collection:* 180/181, 182/183. *Trevor Owen:* 187 (top). *Mike Pope:* 71 (bottom 2). *Bruell Pressbild:* 77. *John Ransom:* 28, 31 (center). *Trevor Rowe:* 118 (bottom), 149 (bottom right). *David Seudamore:* 48 (top), 141 (top), 150/151, 152/153 (all 3). *SNCF:* 11 (top), 86/87 (both), 88 (bottom left). *John Snell:* 37 (center). *South African Railways:* 156, 157 (top). *Brian Stephenson:* 68/69. *Eric Treacy:* 16/17, 62/63 (top), 64/65. *Robert M Tyrrell:* 85 (top). *La Vie du Rail:* 50, 66/67, 92/93 (both), 166/167, 171 (top). *Western Australia Government Railways:* 160/161, 167 (center right). *J N Westwood:* 90/91, 96/97, 99, *Leonard Whalley:* 162 (bottom), 165 (center), 167 (bottom). *C Michael Whitehouse:* 73 (center right), 184/185. *P B Whitehouse Collection:* 14/15 (both), 20/21, 25 (bottom right), 37 (bottom right), 74/75 (both), 76, 89 (both), 114, 158/159, 172/173, 174/175, 177, 178, 186/187. *John Wymond:* 170. *Yorkshire Evening Press:* 16 (top). *Ron Ziel:* 94, 98, 124/125.